ZEN DOODLE
The Art of Zen Doodle

Drawing Guide with Step by Step Instructions
Book one

By Jane McKenty

Table of Contents

Disclaimer

While all attempts have been made to verify the information provided in this book, the author does assume any responsibility for errors, omissions, or contrary interpretations of the subject matter contained within. **The information provided in this book is for educational and entertainment purposes only. The reader is responsible for his or her own actions and the author does not accept any responsibilities for any liabilities or damages, real or perceived, resulting from the use of this information.**

The trademarks that are used are without any consent, and the publication of the trademark is without permission or backing by the trademark owner. All trademarks and brands within this book are for clarifying purposes only and are the owned by the owners themselves, not affiliated with this document.

Introduction

Zen art is available for everyone. It makes you more relaxed, confident, creative, focused ... You do not need previous experience and special materials. For Zen doodling/art, you need a simple pencil, a piece of paper and a desire to draw. The book that is in front of you contains more explanatory pictures than text, so I hope you will have a lot of fun with it.

When I was 16 I found myself in pubescent crisis. Instinctively, I began to draw large exotic flowers filled with various patterns. Patterns, which contained dots, hearts, lines, curves and circles, simply "came out" of me.

Until then I had never heard of Zen art drawing technique, which under this name was not yet even been enthroned, and I drew incredibly large flowers made with exactly this technique. Don't you find it strange?

For me, it is now proof that the Zen doodling technique of drawing is one of the man's primeval ways to bring its world in order while expressing creativity.

Let's roll on a Zen doodling journey by understanding how this technique can do you good regarding your **psychophysical balance.**

Chapter 1 –Zen doodling, the art of meditation

Most of us are familiar with the benefits of meditation, if not through our own experience, then through books or the experience of others. Here are just some of the benefits of meditation, which singled out the American National Health Institute:

- reduced anxiety

- reduced pain

- relieve symptoms of depression

- overcoming insomnia

- reducing the symptoms of chronic diseases such as heart disease,

- cancer, HIV and other

- lowering blood pressure

- slowing the heart speed

- reducing cholesterol levels

- improvement in the flow of air to the lungs

I meditate for many years because I am aware that meditation helps me in everyday life. In classic meditation, while direct the attention to the meditation object, for example, breath, thoughts are constantly rolling in your mind. So after 20 minutes of sitting in a meditative position, you realize that you were thinking all the time. After several months of practice, you'll be able to keep the attention on the object of meditation.

What's great about Zen doodling meditation is that the constant focus on the drawing simply does not allow thoughts to fly all over your mind. As soon as you let the thought rush in your mind, you will make a mistake in drawing. That is a tangible proof that you are lost in thoughts.

When you notice a mistake in the drawing, you will try more to draw well. The more you try the more attention you paid to the entire drawing. Any other thoughts vanish and your mind is clear. What I write is not a scientific fact, but my experience with Zen drawing.

To be free of illness, we have to empty our mind of fear and worry and to understand how the disease is the result of wrong thinking. With a Zen method of drawing you can:

- relax

- record daily feelings

- improve sleep and overcome insomnia

- increase self-confidence

- develop inspiration

- overcome panic attacks

- improve behavior

- create beautiful works of art

- get stress relief

- improve motor skills

- exercise eyesight

- improve the ability to focus

Just don't be like those people who constantly talk and read about meditation, and never had empirically tested it. For this reason, take a paper and a marker and let's start!

Chapter 2-For a Start

For start, things you will need so you could draw Zen doodles or patterns inspired by Zentangle official patterns are as follows:

- The thicker white copy paper

- Felt-tip pens or markers of different thickness

- lead pencil

- Eraser for lead pencil

- Straightedge

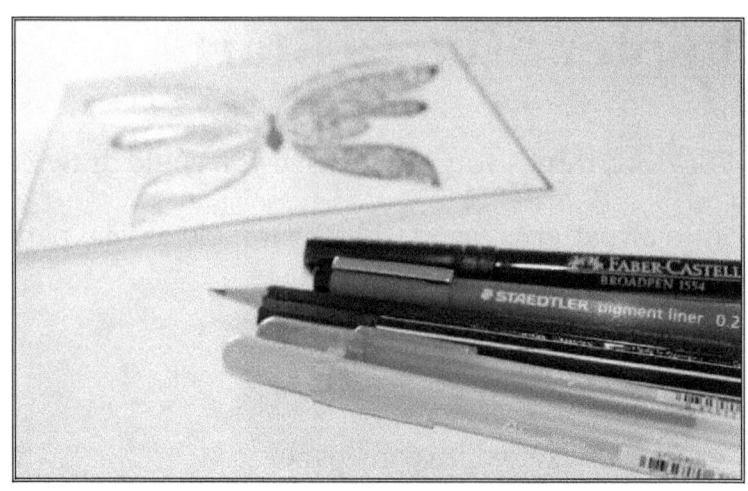

As the additional material, you can use different shape rulers-straight, round or those for children that come in various forms. Also, you can use different sizes plugs, molds for cakes or even your own hand.

The official form of the tile that you will draw on is the white paper in a form of a square with each side length of 9 cm. First time you can use a ruler to draw tiles, but soon it will not be required because you'll get used to drawing geometric shapes freehand.

After you have created your base for drawing, enjoyment can begin. You can cut some cardboard measures as the tile, which will serve as a model for the tile. This part of the paper, by the way, is called tile in Zen drawing because more tiles can be combined into a mosaic.

You can easily buy kits for Zen drawings that include the best quality paper tiles and corresponding pencils. One of the beautiful ideas is that you can even make a scrapbook out of your Zen doodles. It would be something like a diary of your art and emotions.

Chapter 3 – Zen doodle patterns

In this chapter we will be dealing with variations of official Zentangle patterns and the first one is a pattern I named simply a **Chess Board** which is based on a Zentangle pattern called Knightsbridge.

Chess Board

One of the basic Zentangle ornaments is called Knightsbridge. This pattern, like all the other patterns, has endless customizing alternatives. Also, this simple framework is the basis for many other advanced patterns. Once you master the straight on the grid, you can wriggle the lines and change things. When coloring in squares, you should color the square that is rubbing the corner of the one you have just colored.

That is, by the way, one of my favorite basic patterns so I change it by adding some lines. Each of us draws at least once something like that. Classic Knightsbridge is a black-and-white pattern, but it certainly can be painted with various colors, as you can see on the picture below. Your chess board can be also cracked as on the 4th picture. The 5th picture shows another variation of a chess board that includes a square shape with a dot inside the blank grids.

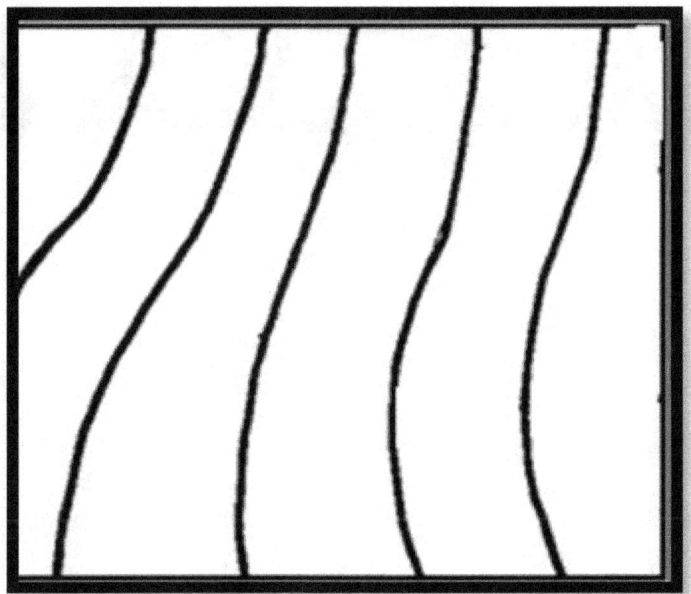

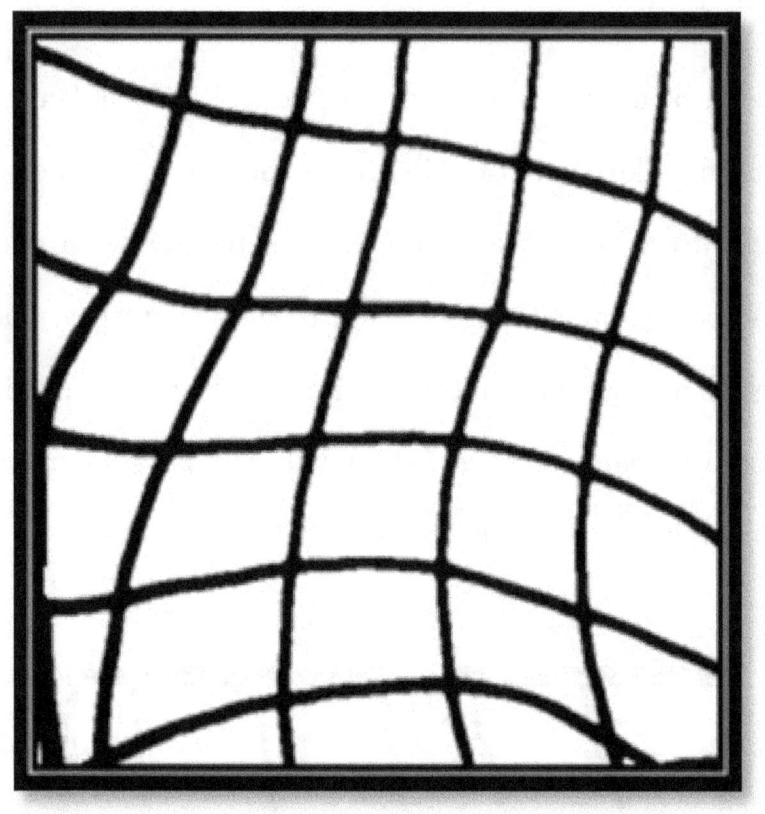

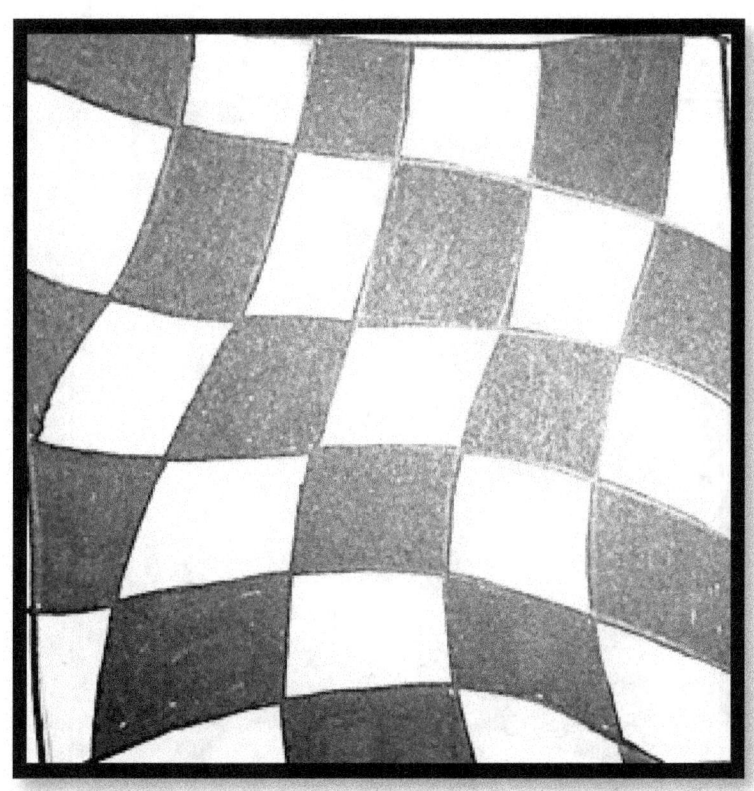

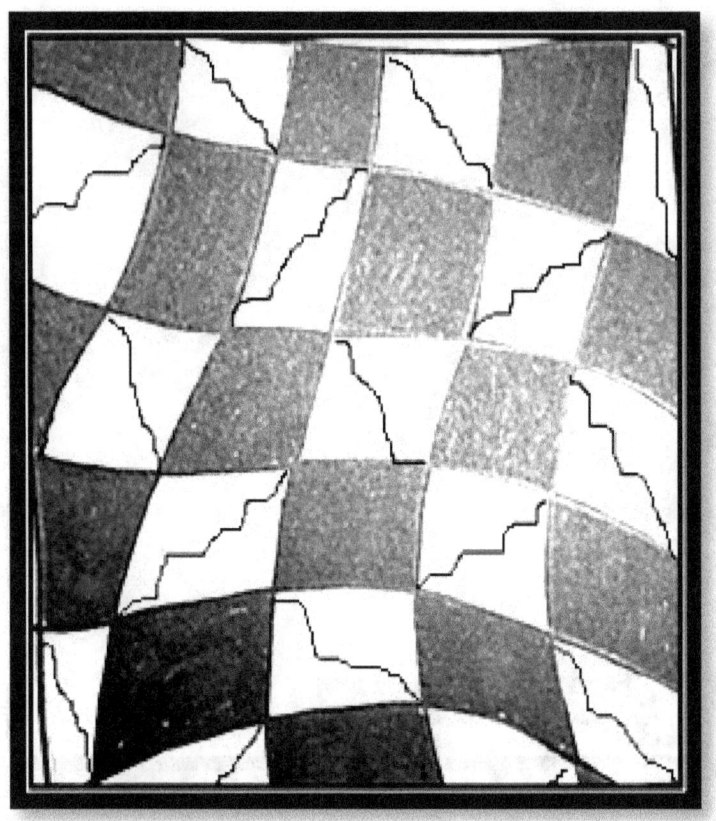

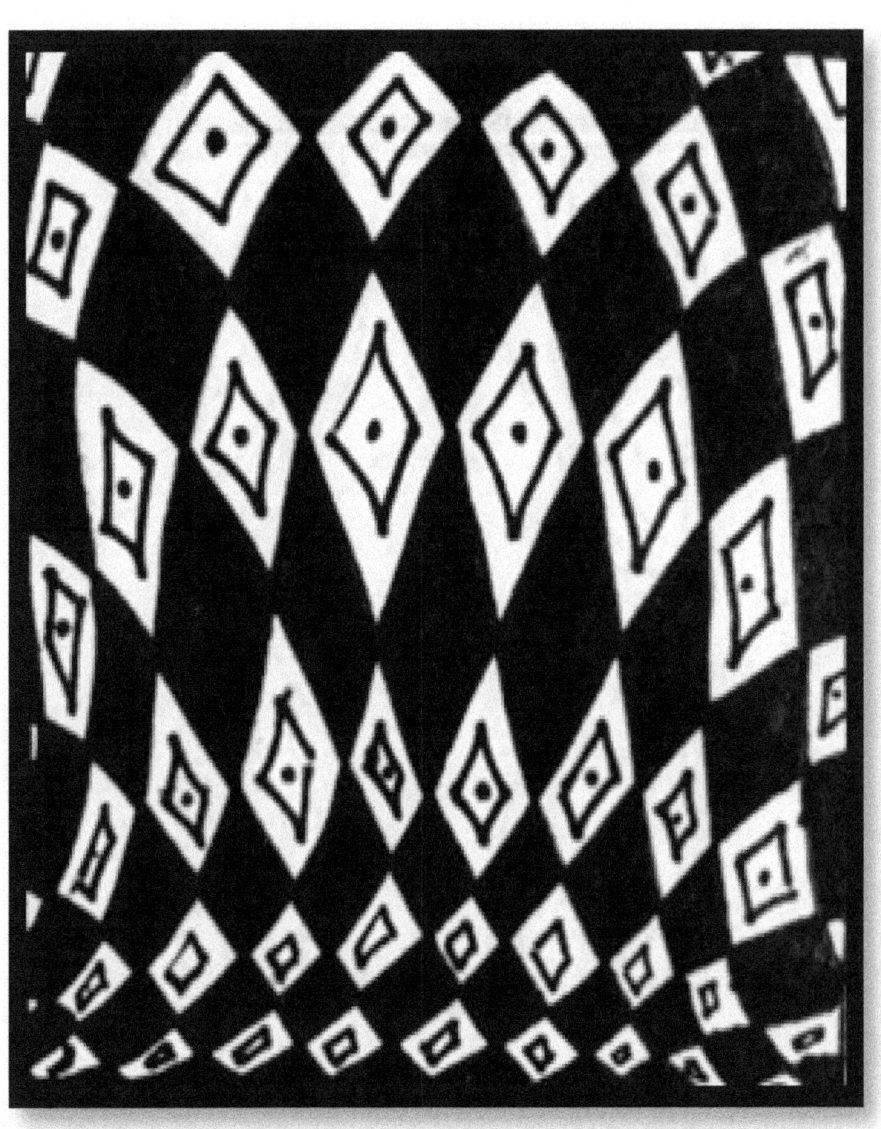

World

This Zen pattern of mine is also encouraged with Knightsbridge. On this first picture, you can see how it all began. I will leave to your imagination to guess why I named it like this. It's all started as pulled curtains, and everything else is my sub consciousness speaking.

You can see from the pictures below how it was all developing. I have doodled whatever came to my mind, from full dots and triangles to empty dots and curved lines.

You can copy what I have drawn or you will most likely be carried away by your own imagination, so this can be just a starting point.

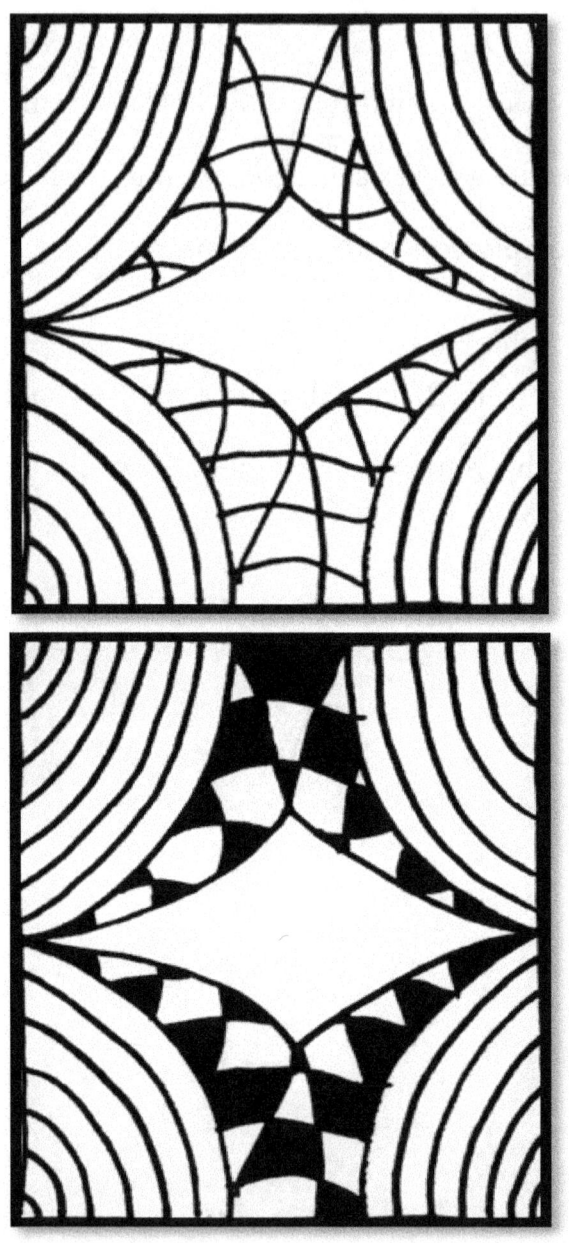

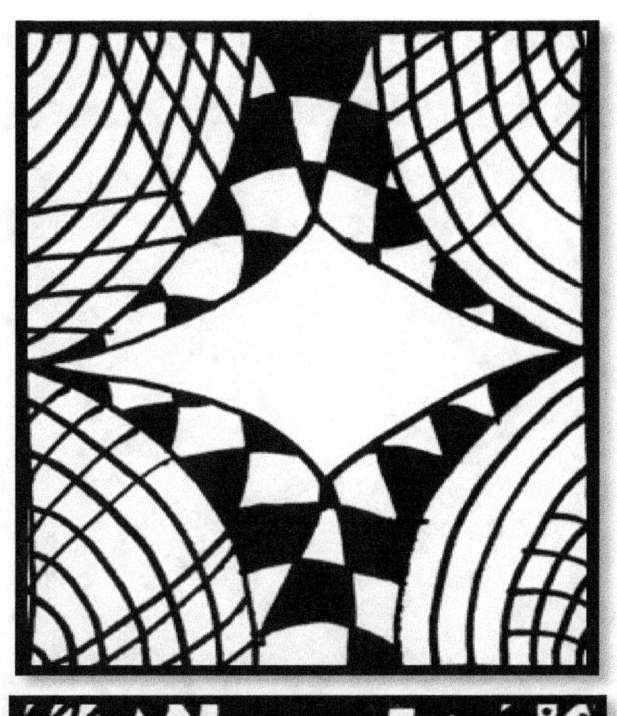

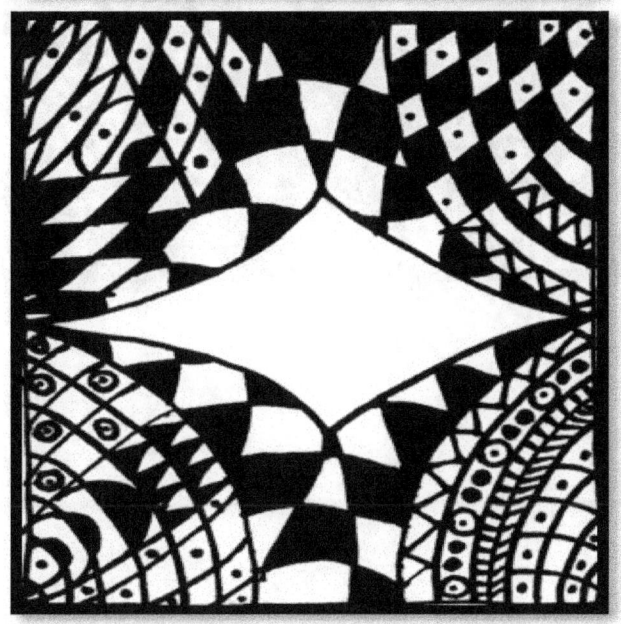

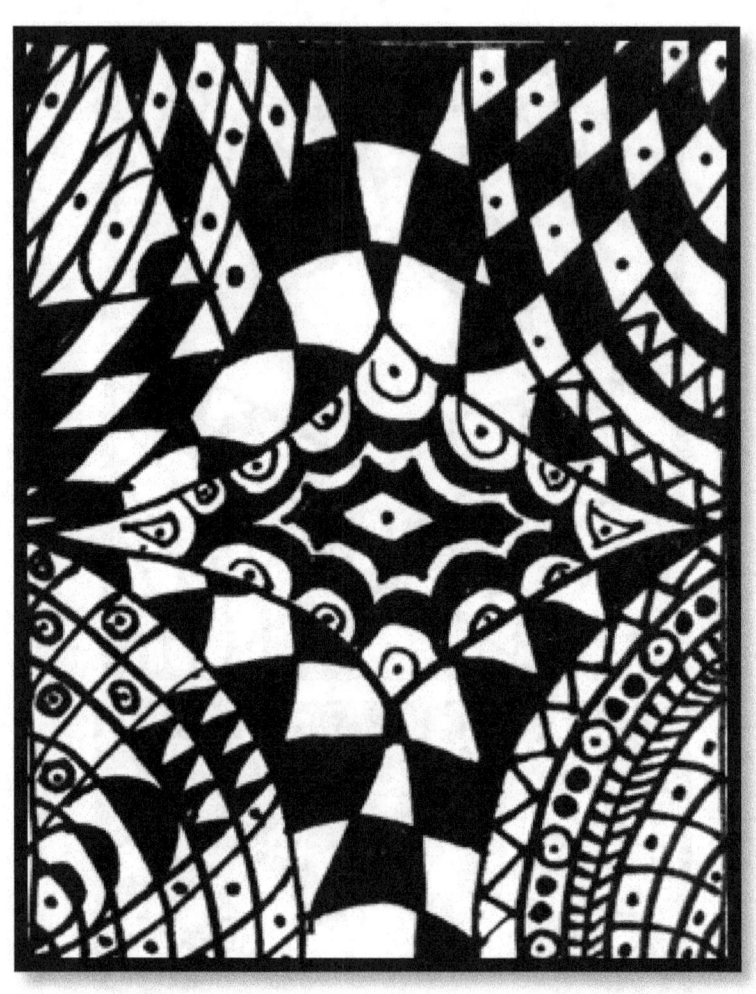

Gran

I got the inspiration to draw Gran by exercising one of the official patterns called Bales. Bales are one of the official patterns created and introduced by Maria Thomas, Rick Roberts and Molly Hollibaugh, founders of Zentangle©. First, draw a field as shown below. If you are a beginner, it is best to use a ruler. Then draw two crossed diagonals from the corner to corner. Then on each side of two main diagonals add 3 more. Now you have a total of 7 struts on each side.

Then turn to petals. Be careful, no matter how easy it may look-just a moment of carelessness is enough for you to mess up. Don't forget the dots.

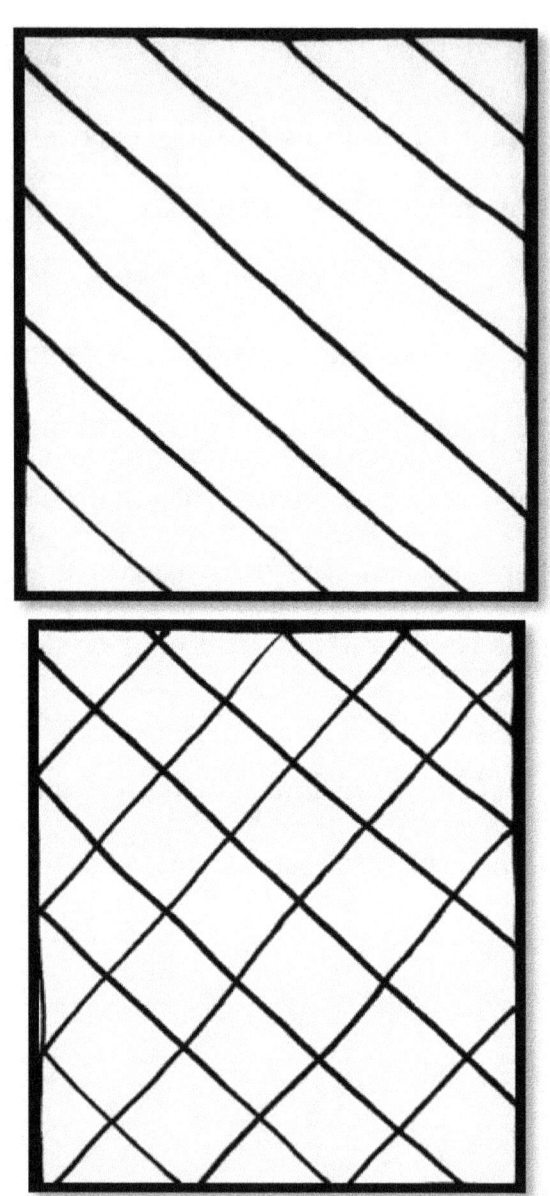

Empty dots/small circles are in the middle of something that reminds me of granny's bun. Of course, this pattern, as well as the others, is only the basis for expressing your creativity. So, in the last picture you can see how my imagination worked as I painted some of the parts and in some other parts I draw triangles, but you can see a model in it.

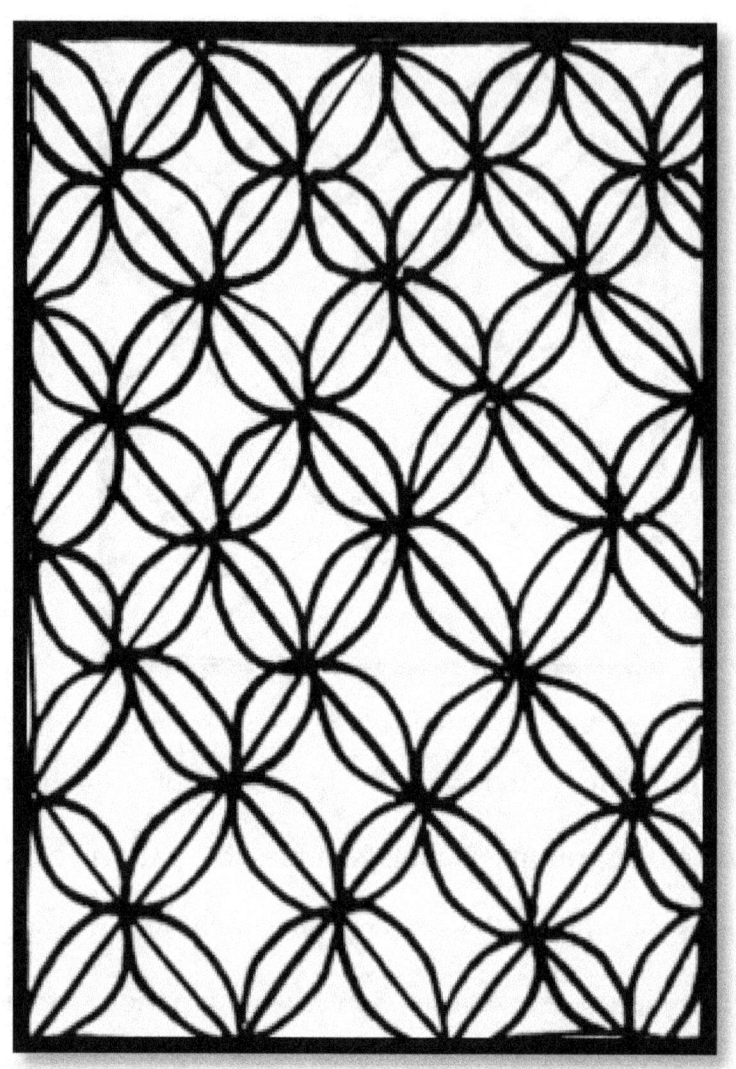

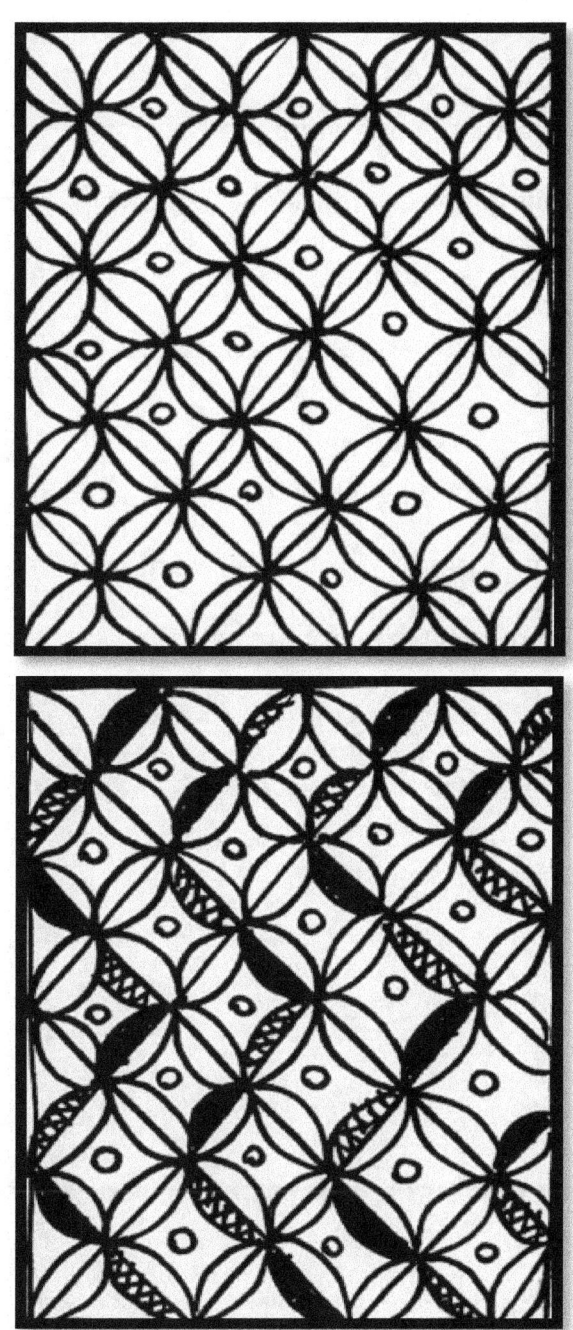

Labyrinth

I have named this model simply a Labyrinth as it looks like that at first sight. It resembles the famous patterns such as Ambler and Emingle. Emingle is a variation of Ambler pattern. You can make your own original variation as I did.

You will find very engaging to draw a labyrinth since you really have to be focused if you don't want to miss the starting point of a line in each of the following squares.

At the beginning, draw a field on the tile using a ruler as shown in the first picture below. The most of the Zen drawings start this way by drawing a field. The first "spiral square" starts when you draw a line from the upper left to the upper right corner. Following Square starts also from the upper left corner, but goes to the bottom left corner and the next one from the bottom right corner to the bottom left corner. All in all, you are forming lines in the opposite direction from clockwise. Look carefully at the picture below to catch the method.

When you finish drawing with pencil, bold the lines using thinner marker. Since this is a square spiral, be careful not to get carried away and draw a circular spiral. By the way, this pattern actually helps me the most in increasing concentration.

As you can notice on the last picture, you can fill in the square that is in the center. The first line is bolded so you can easily see from where to start.

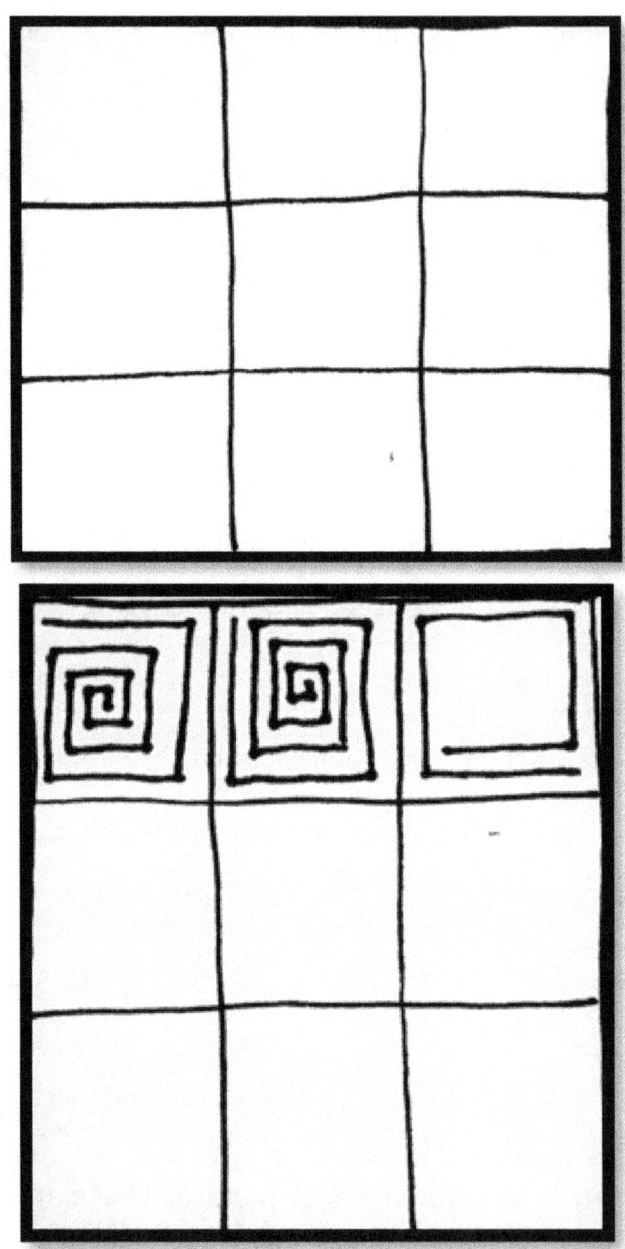

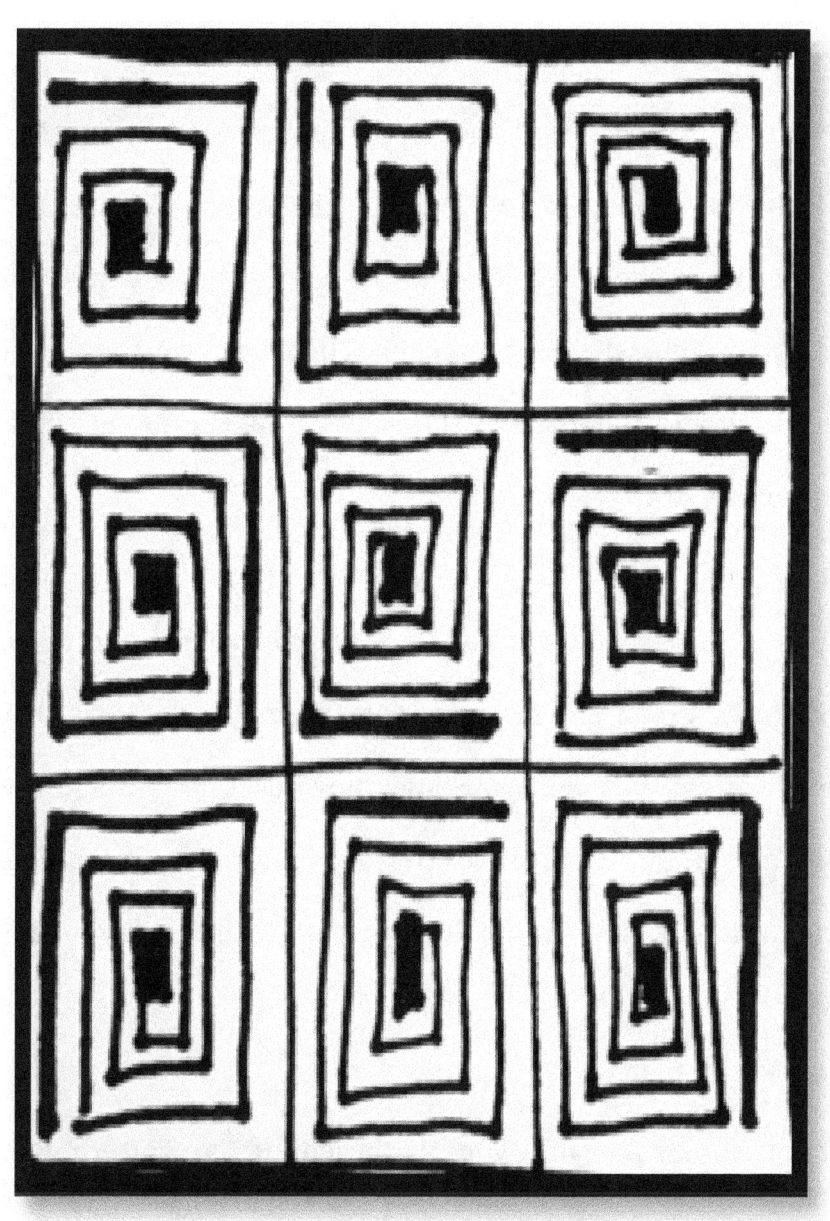

Snowflake

Snowflake is one of the easiest patterns to draw and it resembles a famous pattern called Aah. As you can see, I am not that inventive when it comes to names, I see a snowflake and not an Aah, whatever it means. The important thing for us is to draw and meditate at the same time, the names of the patterns are not very important.

As a beginner, you should use a graphite pencil and eraser. First draw 5 or 6 small circles with a pencil. Note that each snowflake has 8 tentacles. Some snowflakes are smaller and some are larger. You can draw this pattern, both with and without dots, which in this drawing resemble the snow falling down.

Take a look below how you can enrich the Aah pattern.

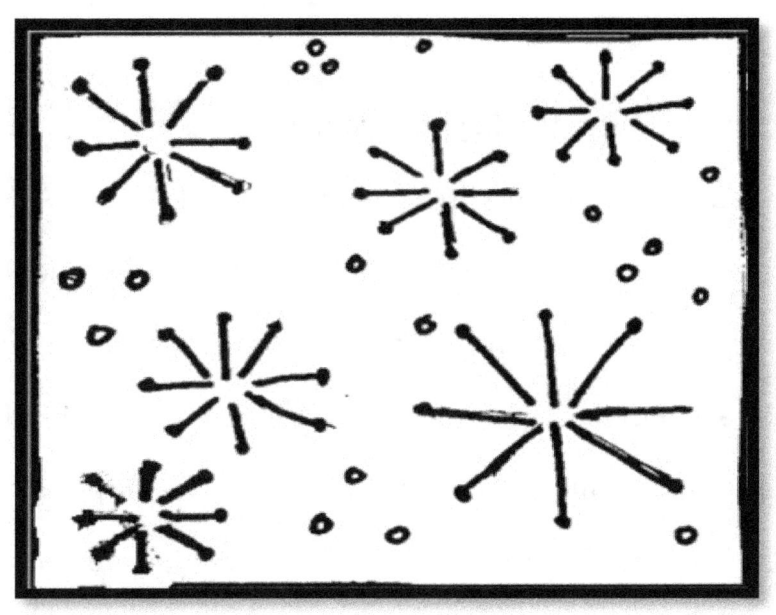

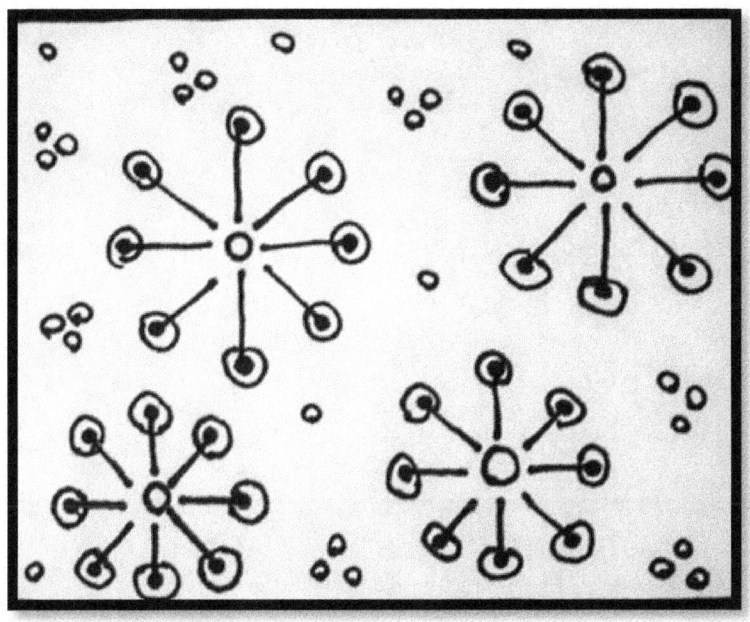

Ra

Ra, named **after the Egyptian sun god,** is a variation of one more famous Zentangle© patterns that is called Arucas. Ra is also great for beginners. First, draw a circle in the middle of the tile and bold it with a marker. Then outline tentacles, which should be symmetrical, with an ordinary ruler. Tentacles are composed of irregular rectangles. After, add the diffuse in opposite directions lines as shown on the 4th picture. Do not forget to rotate the tile while you're drawing.

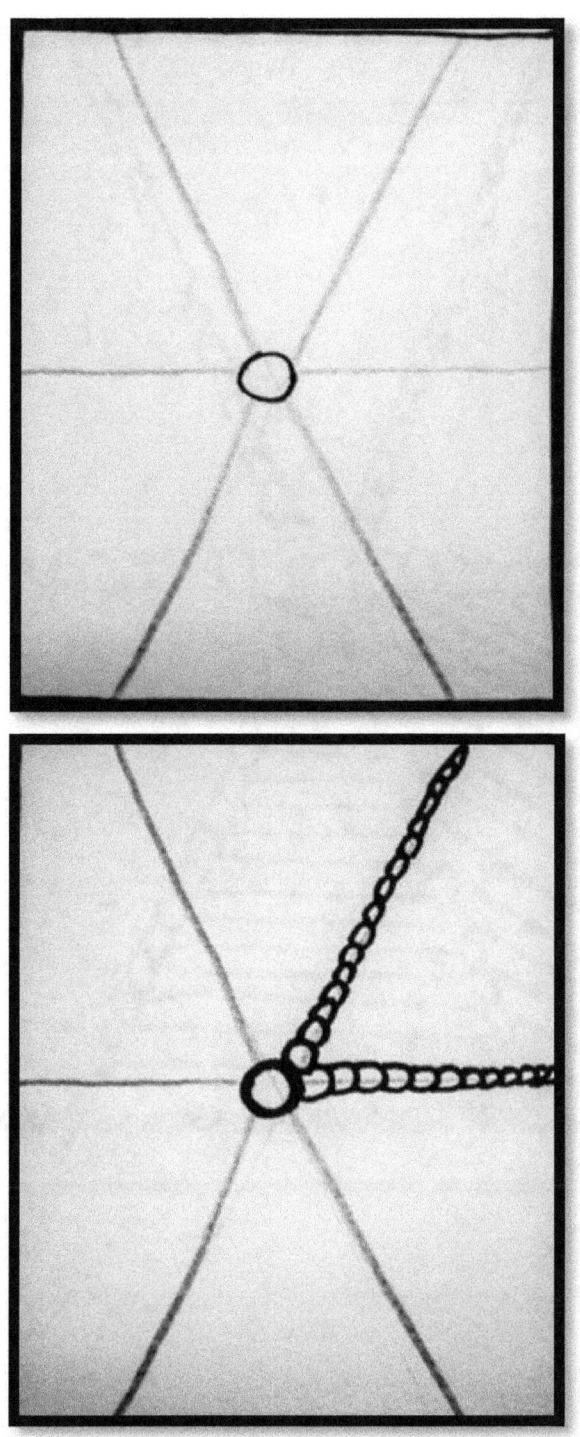

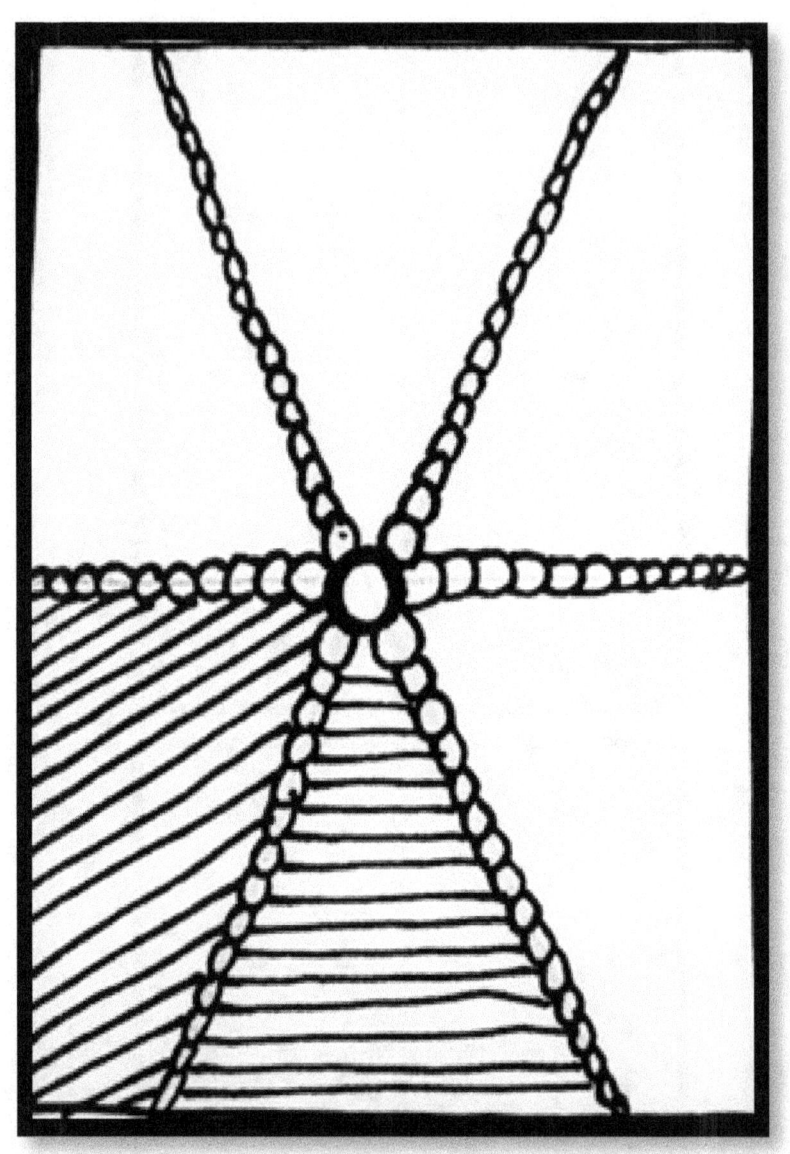

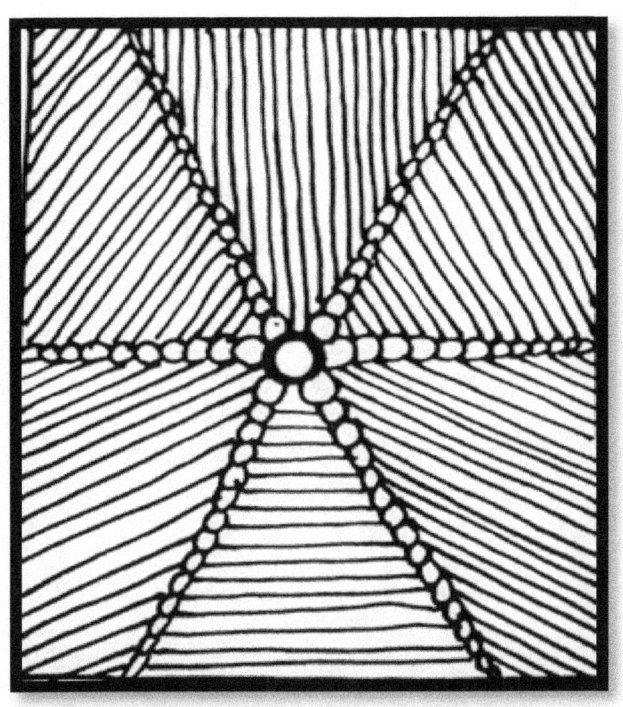

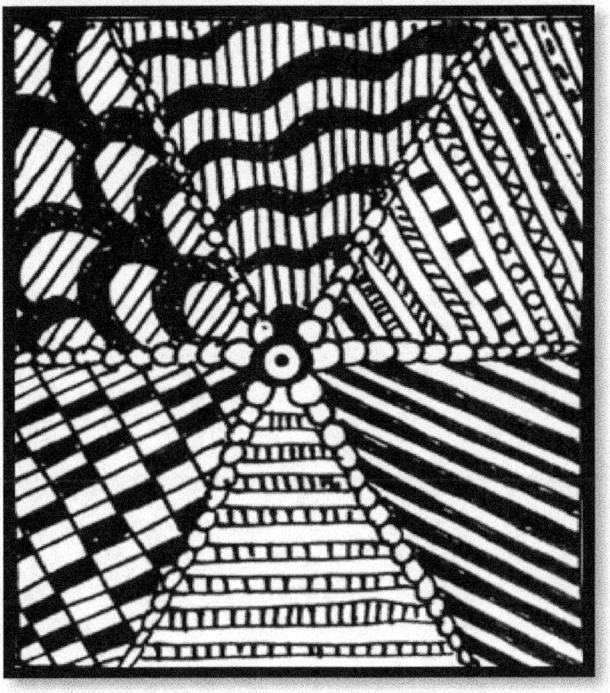

On the 5th picture, you can see I didn't draw Arucas, but I used other various ways to fill in the gaps between the branches of a figure. You can draw an identical pattern or you can allow your imagination to take you to some other forms. This book is, anyway, designed more in a way to stimulate your creativity than to give you firm prescriptions.

Speller

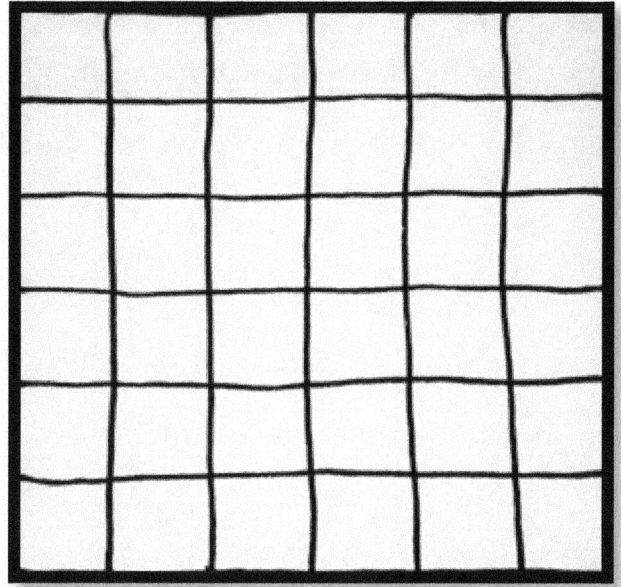

Do you like challenges? If the answer is yes, then you will really enjoy this one inspired by Zen art. I called it the Speller because you will use the first letters of the alphabet to draw it. First, draw a field with five vertical and five horizontal lines. If you are not very good in technical drawing, I sincerely advice you to measure the tile and use a ruler-otherwise you will have to draw and erase for about hundred times as I did when I first wanted to draw this pattern. It wasn't just about meditating, but it also taught me how to be patient.

You can draw a grid with a graphite pencil and then erased it when you got the pattern, or you can leave the grids so you could add something more that comes to your mind on your Zen doodle.

You will begin with 4 A letters from the center of the tile (first three pictures). Next, just follow the images below and enjoy. This pattern is perfect for practicing patience, which we all more or less are missing. And don't forget-rotate the tile permanently, otherwise you will make a blunder.

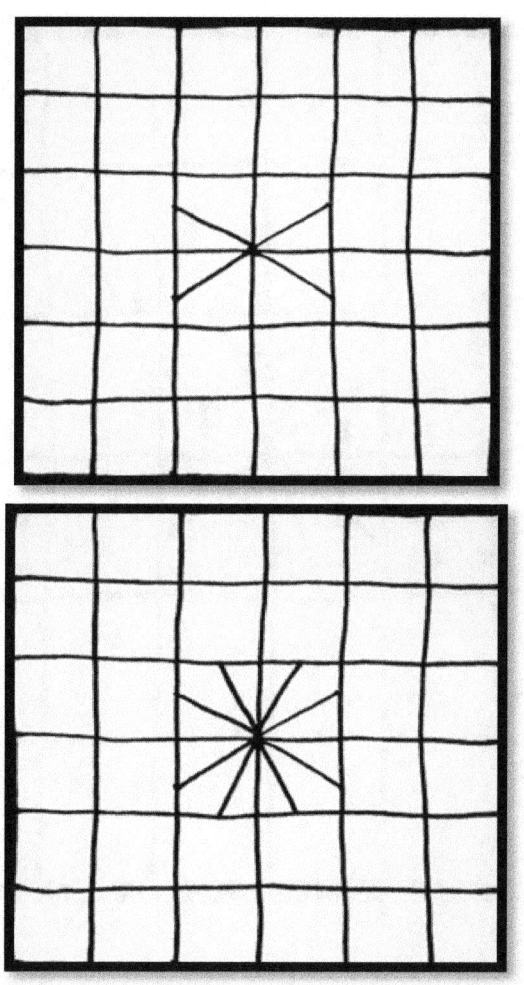

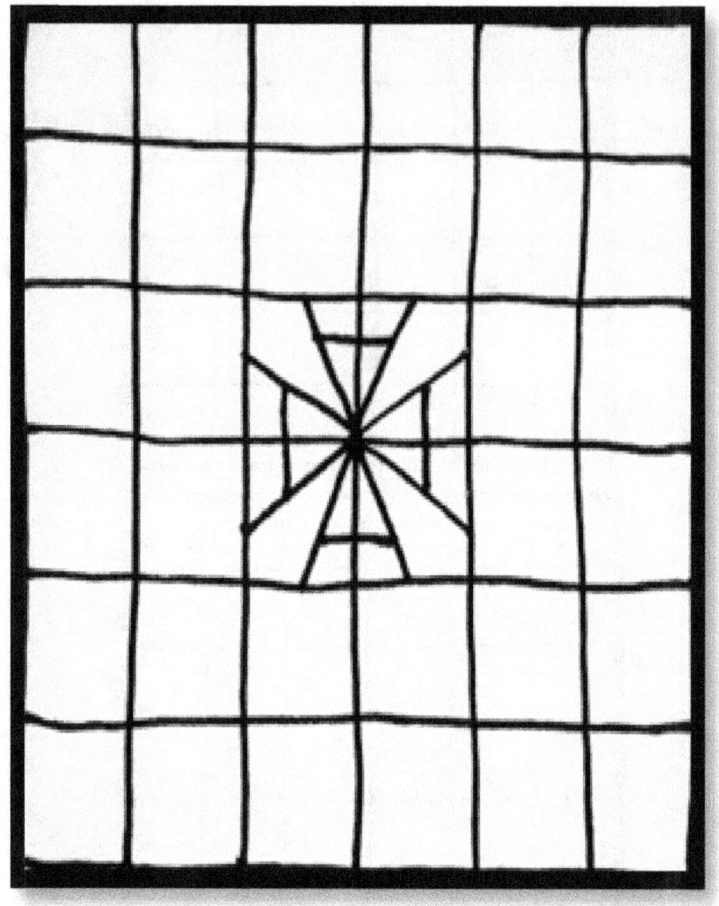

After, just connect the gaps between the A letters (4th picture). These connecting lines will be a starting line for 4 B letters as shown on the 5th picture. Next, you will draw the letter C as on the 6th picture below.

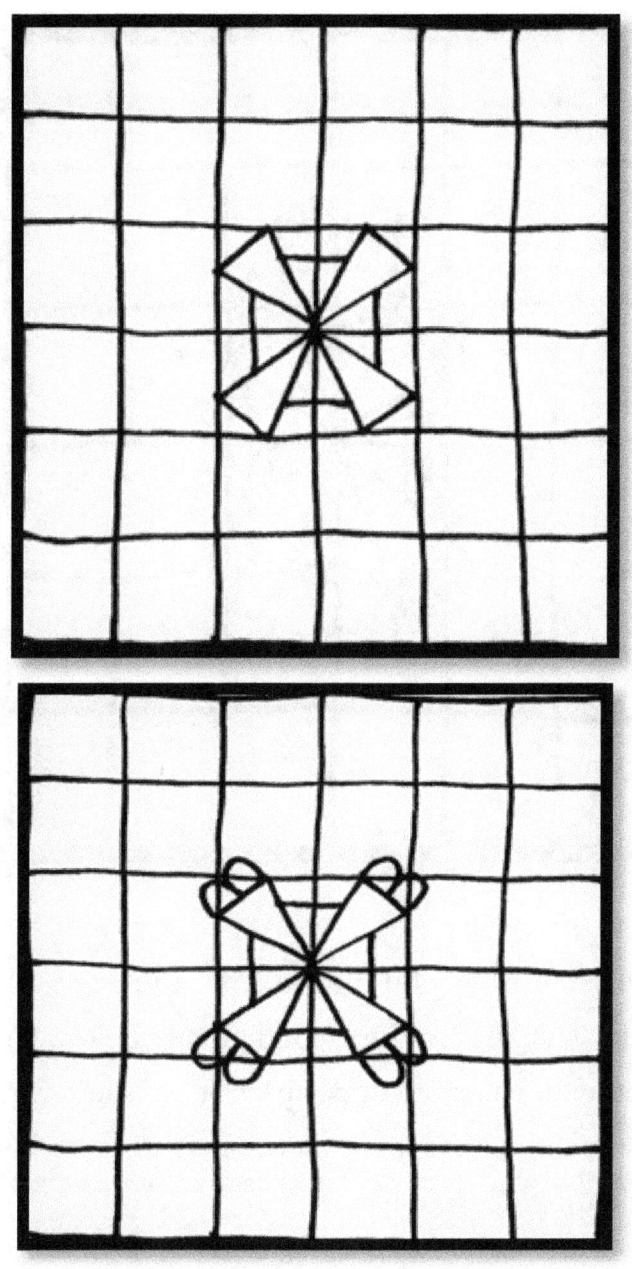

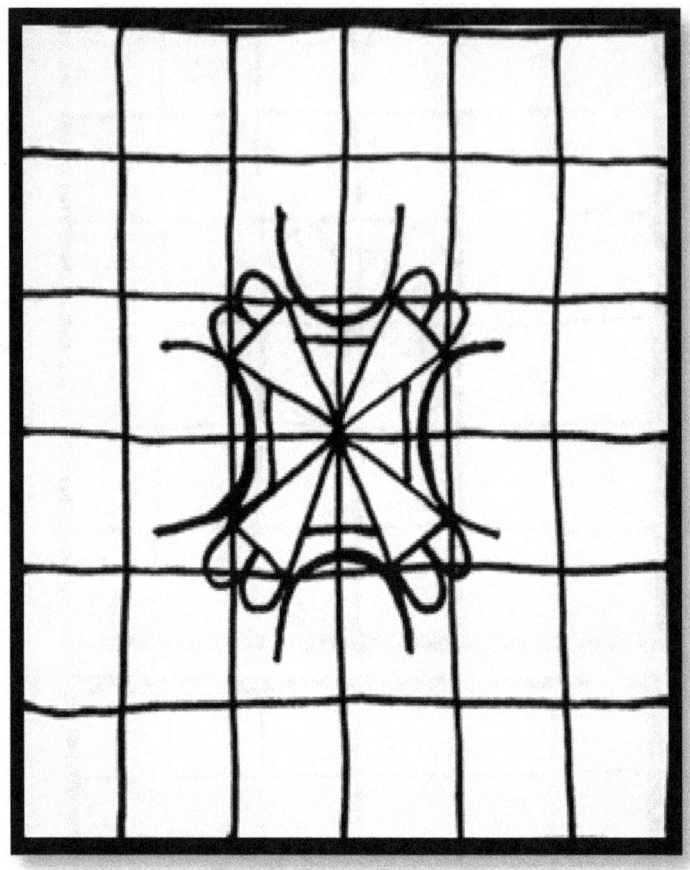

Now, just pull those little lines from the edges of a tile to draw a letter A again. On the second picture below, you can see how I filled with color the upper part of an A letter. As before, you will now draw a B letter whenever is needed, just look at the third picture below.

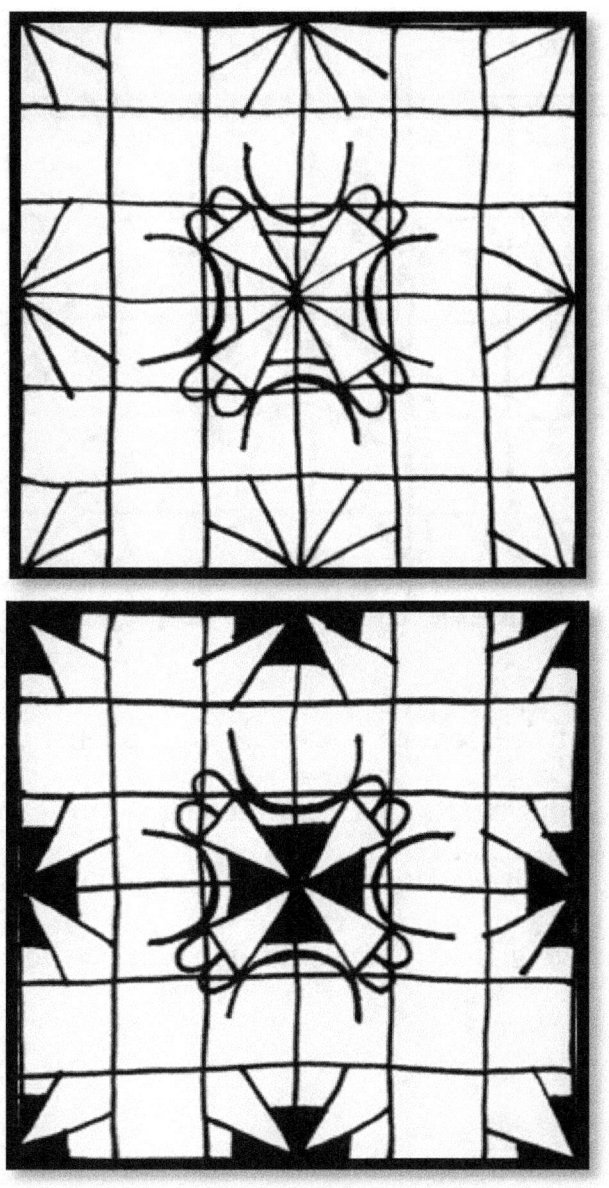

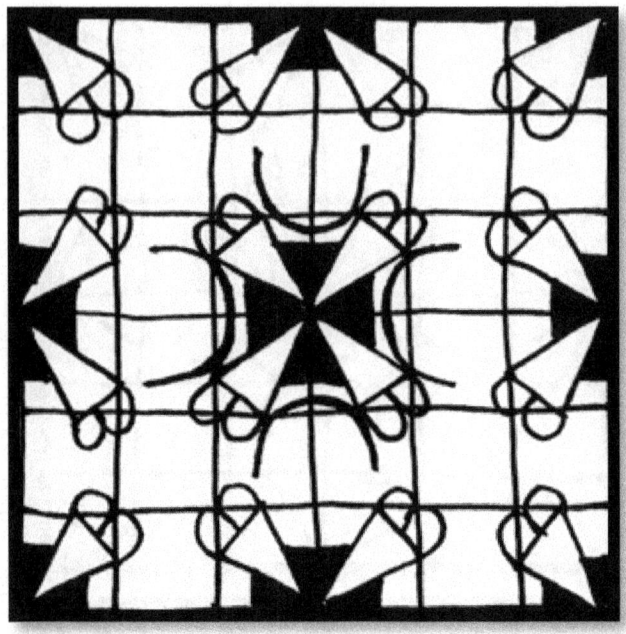

Because of the Zen art patterns like a Speller, we can say that with all our hearts that Zen drawing is a true meditation. You will need all your focus to draw something like this and believe me every lack of concentration will be shown on your Zen doodle.

You can now connect the C letters so they look like a tulip and you can fill the B letters with the net like I did so they look like an ice cream. On the last picture you can see a variation of a Speller pattern where I have erased the grid with whom I started at the first place.

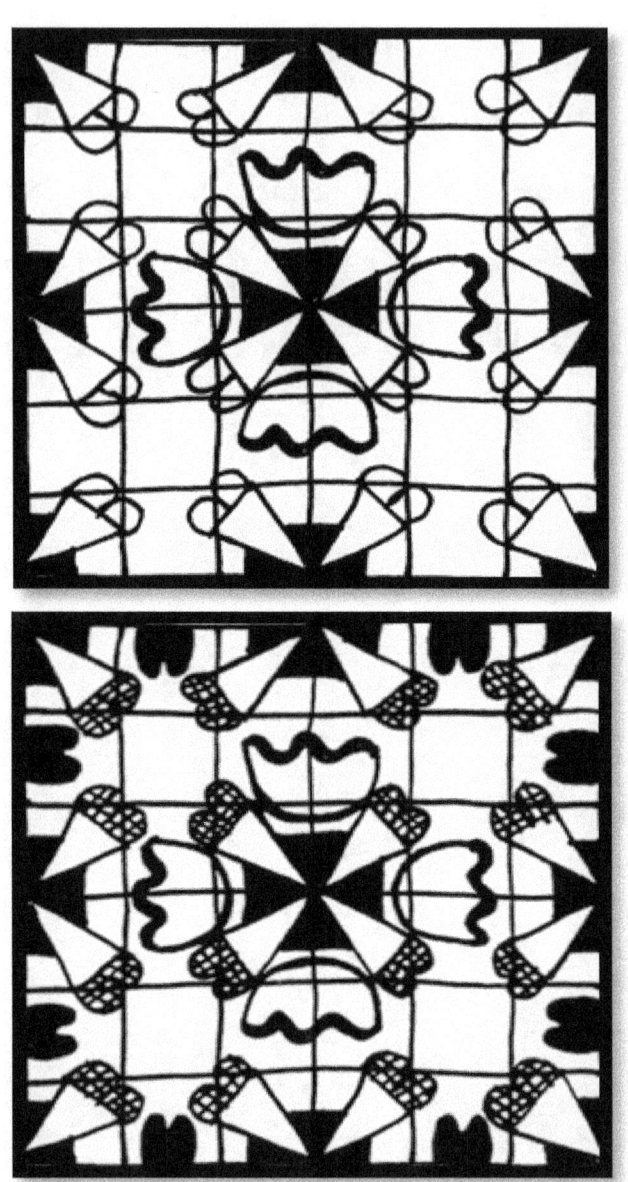

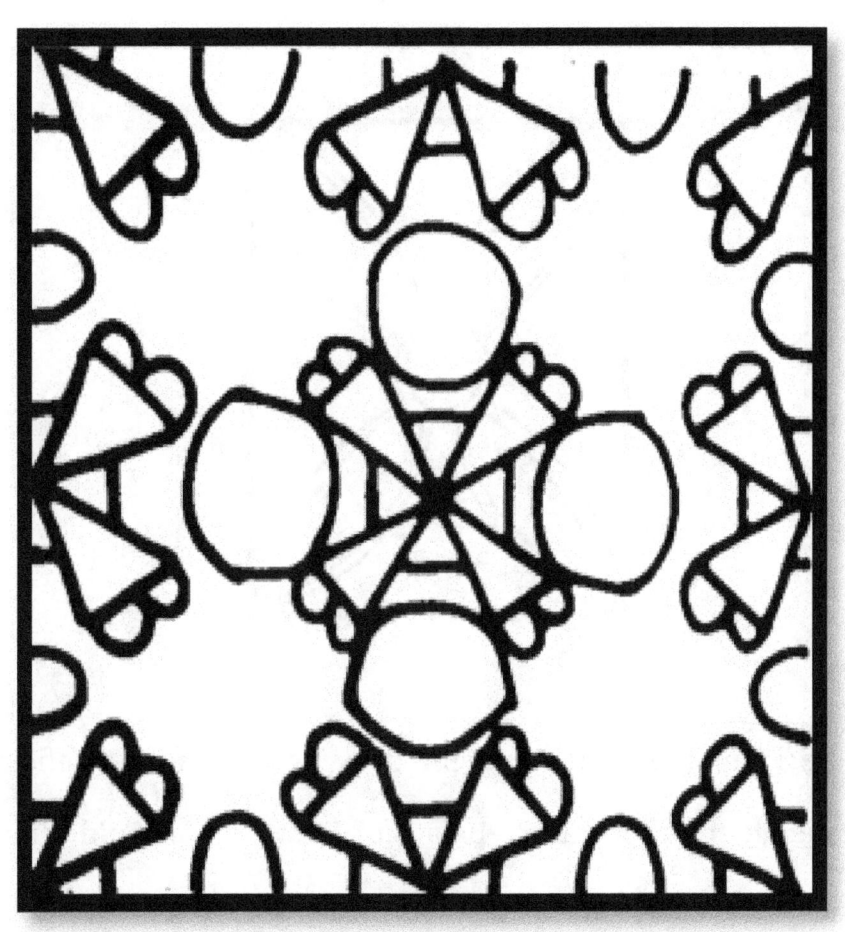

Bunny

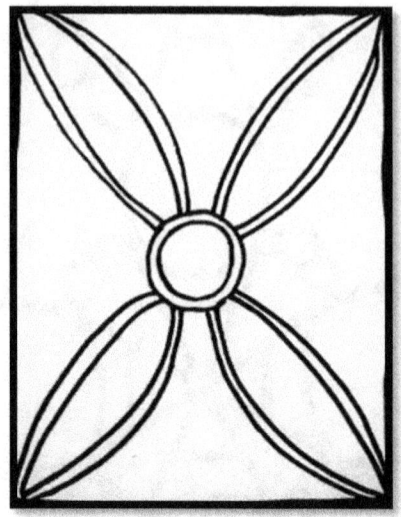

Here is another pattern inspired by flowers and an official Zentangle pattern called Balawat. First, you should draw pestle with 4 petals in the middle of the tile. You should draw 4 large petals with double lines. After that, you will draw 4 "realistic" flowers between the large petals. They look like crowns. You'll have to turn the tile constantly if you wish to make it beautiful.

I chose to fill out large petals with "fish scales". Maybe because I'm a Pisces, who knows? As I've already mentioned: sub consciousness is speaking through our Zen drawings. At the end, I've added "an eye" in the middle of a pestle. When I finished it, it reminded me so much of a scared bunny so I called it that way: **Bunny**.

As you can see you have a lot of blank space to express your creativity. It doesn't have to end this way. Here is another variation on the third picture.

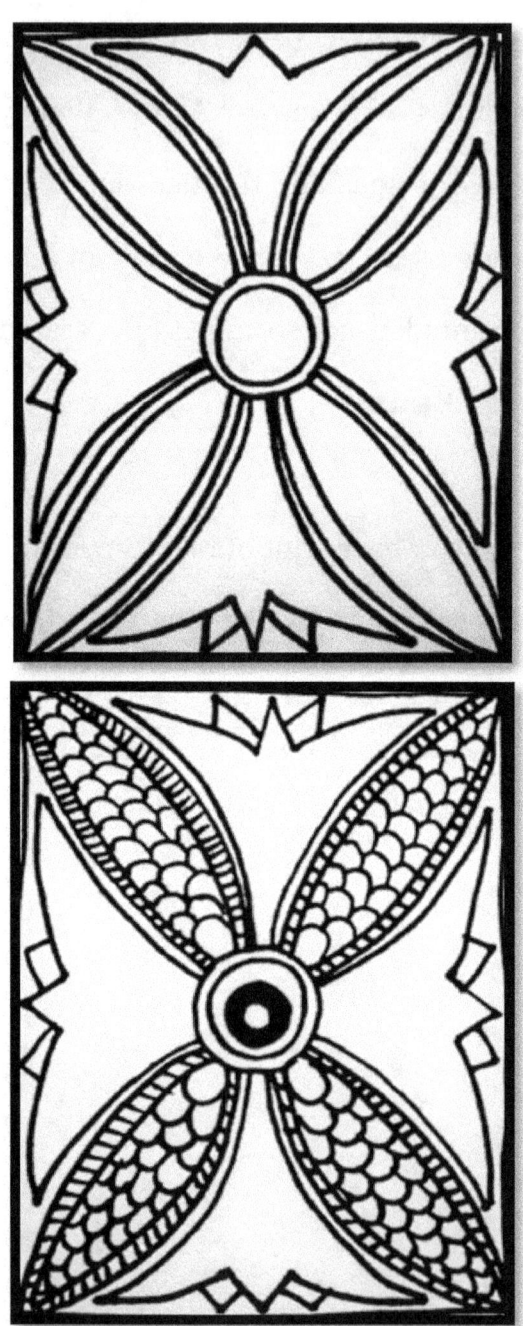

Sea Angel

This pattern is outstanding, you can truly make an artistic picture with this for your living room, I sure did since I found it truly fantastic and easy to make. Draw a longer curve line in the middle of the tile with a "head ", as shown in the picture below. It looks like a distorted nail. Then add 4 more of the same curves to the left side and three on the right.

Connect the "heads" with curve lines as shown in the picture and shade it with a lead pencil or a marker. It's so beautiful and easy to draw.

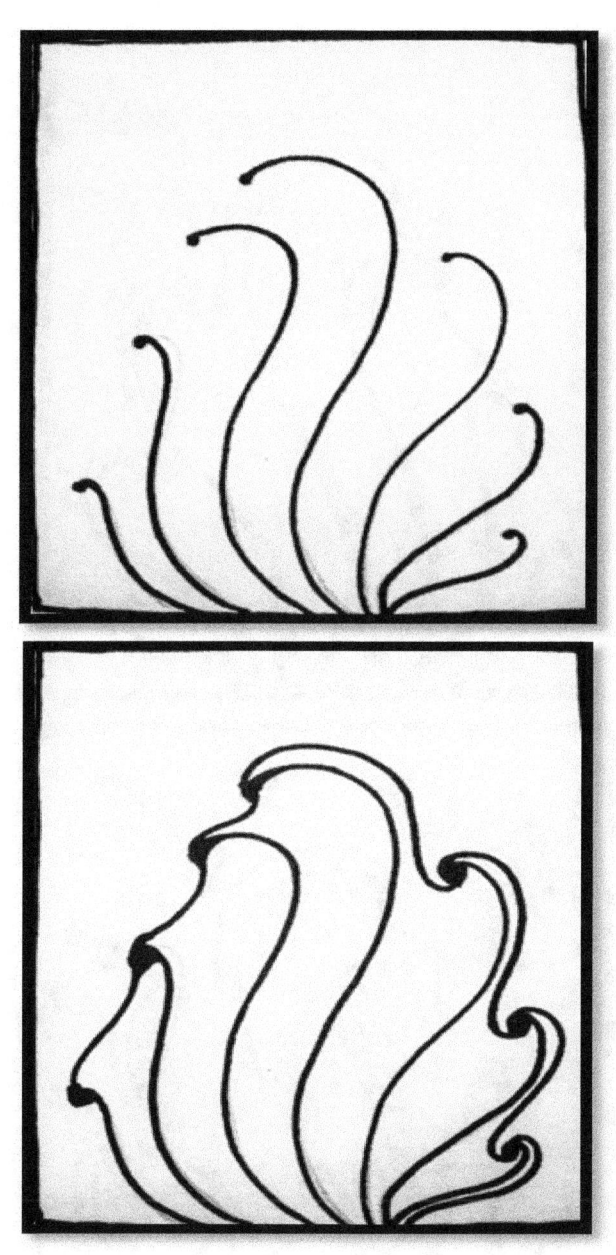

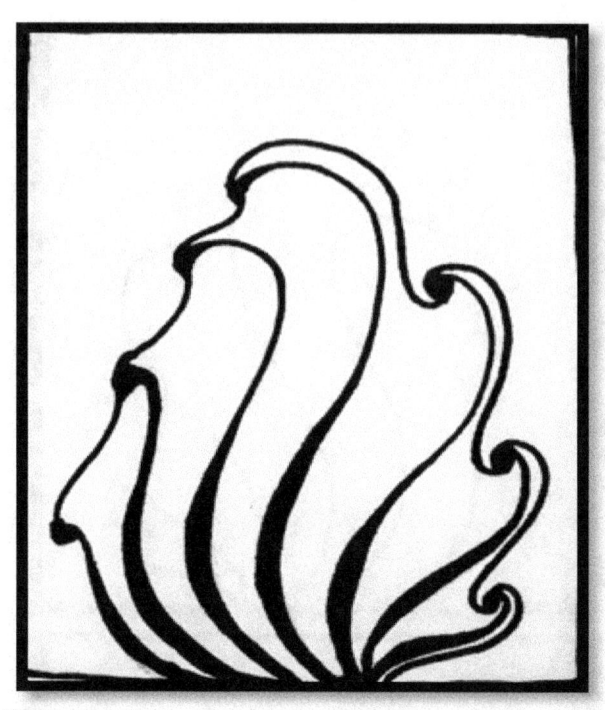

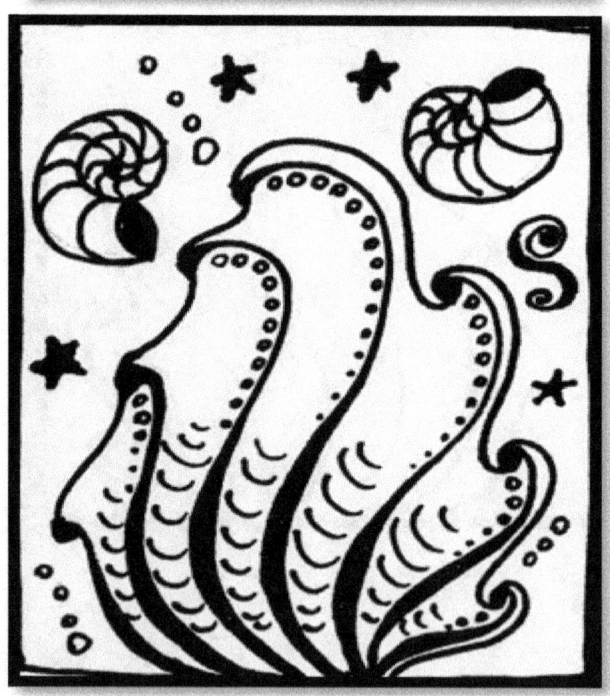

Now, my true creativity comes to the fore. I've added some really cute seashells and filled stars and water bubbles. You can copy it to get this beautiful Zen drawing. I personally, wouldn't add anything else; it looks perfect as it is.

Diamante

This pattern is inspired by a well-known Zen pattern called Hitched. I suppose it is obvious why I called it a Diamante. It looks like some sort of jewelry to me, a bracelet. I guess it's because I like making handmade jewelry.

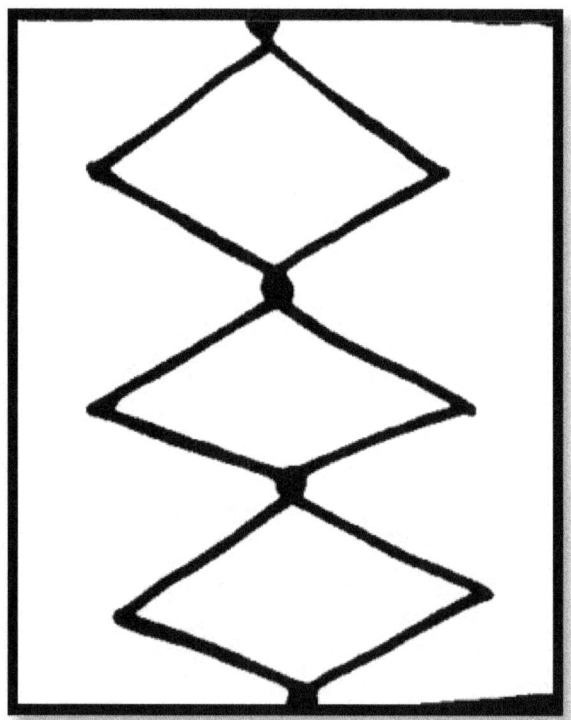

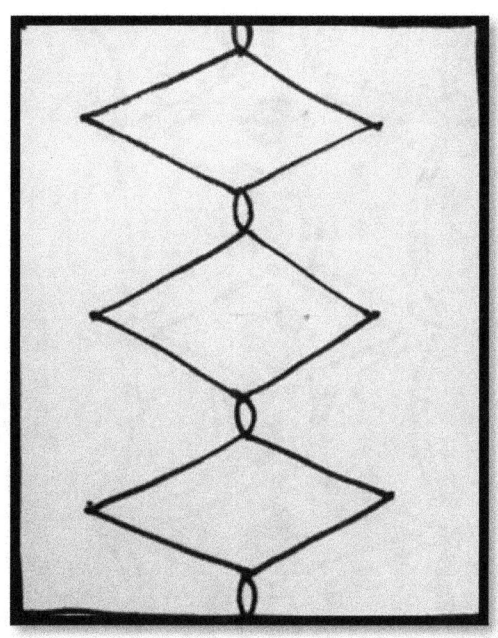

Draw 4 black dots or small circles in the middle of the tile and connect them with lines as on the pictures above so you get 3 rhombuses.

Then add the following three semicircular lines on each side of dots and connect the corners of rhombuses with double semicircular lines. Finally, fill rhombuses as shown in the picture below and shade the external line.

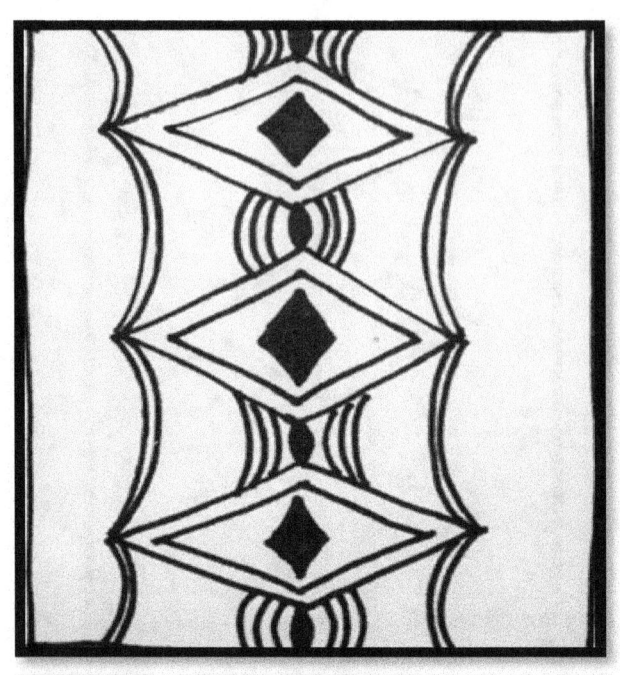

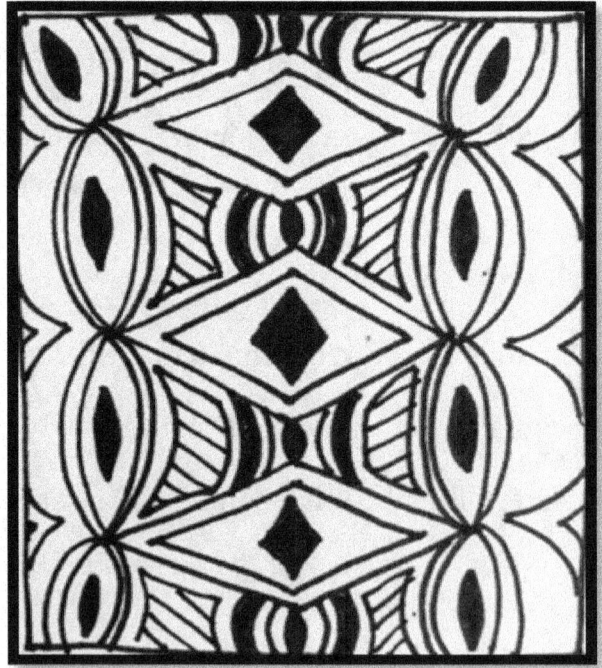

Spotty dotty

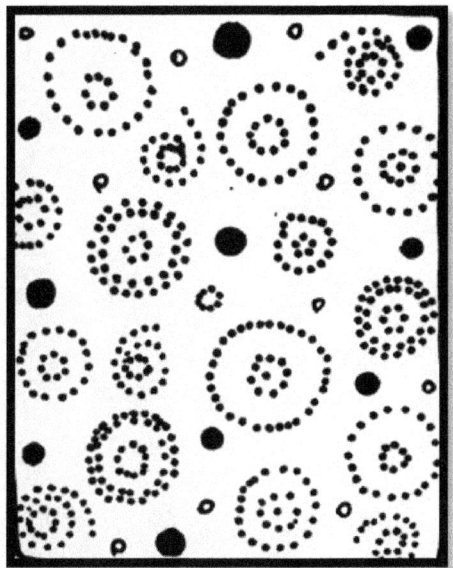

This pattern is not as easy as it looks at first sight. It is a variation of a Raindotty. To draw circles with a lead pencil, you can use a penny or a flat part of the pen. You will, of course, when you have finished drawing delete all traces of the pen.

What you need to pay attention is that there are more dot pitches in a larger circle than in the smaller one.

You will see later how you can combine some of these patterns to make your own Zen drawing.

Darnel

I've always admired a Zen pattern called Persian Flower Knot, so I've decided to make my own version and name it Darnel. This pattern looks kind of creepy to me, do not ask me why, and that is why I chose to call it Darnel.

Again, arm yourself with patience as this really is the tough one, but it pays off after you glance at your work of art. As I said at the beginning, you don't need to know how to draw to make a genuine art with Zen doodling.

This is such a beautiful pattern by itself; you don't have to add anything after. Again, you should draw a field out of squares that you will erase when you're finished. Just follow the pictures from left to right and don't forget you should constantly rotate the tile while drawing. Patience is a must.

As you can see, there is a specific pattern for every shape, like those curved lines and dots on the pictures below.

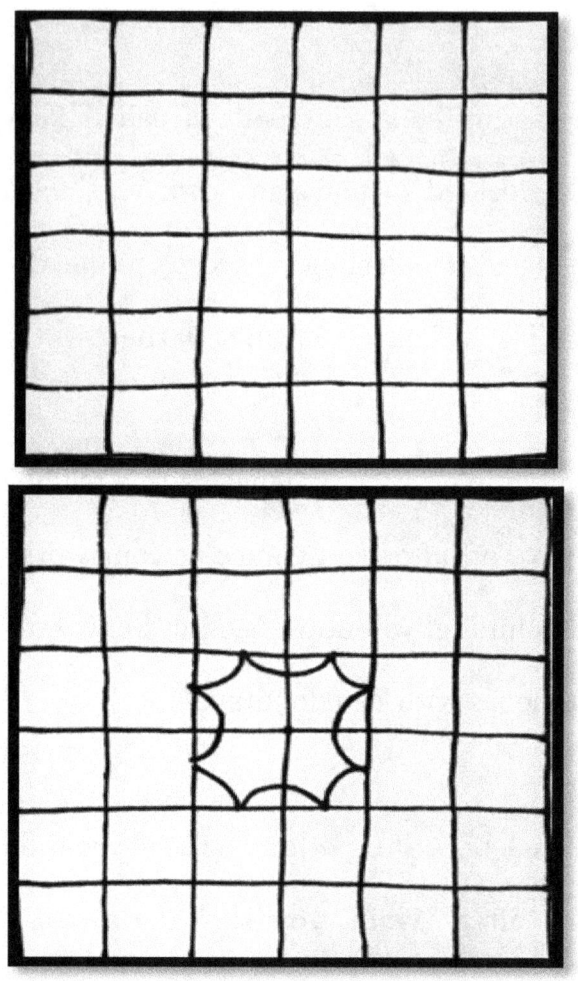

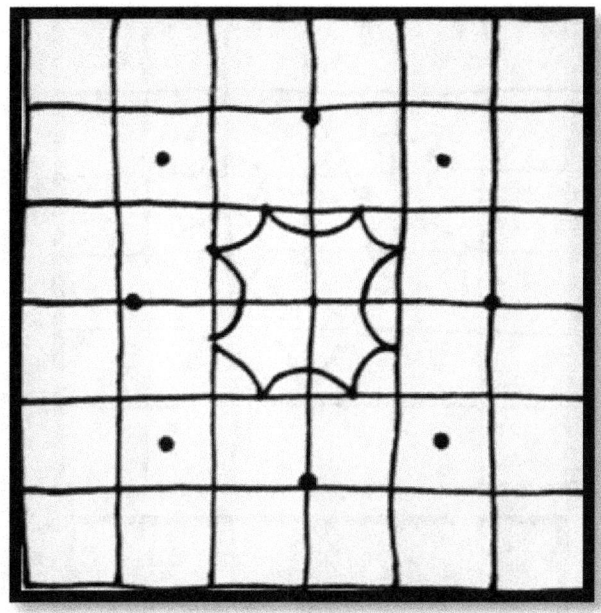

These pictures below are the best explanation you can get,
just look carefully in my drawings and you can't miss anything.

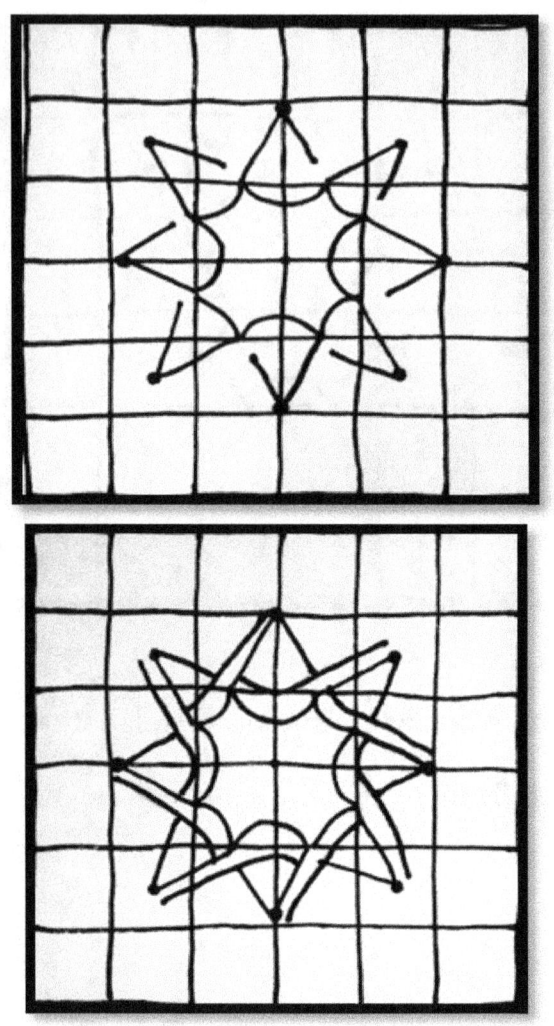

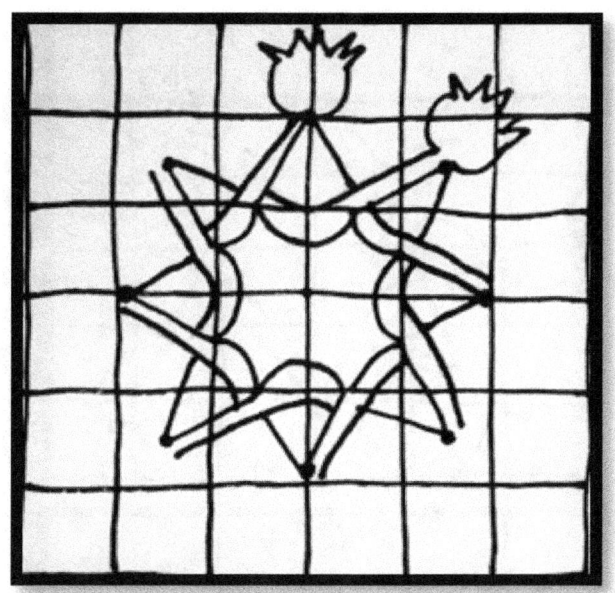

Now, when I look at my drawings, I am tempted to color these "onions" in a passionate red.

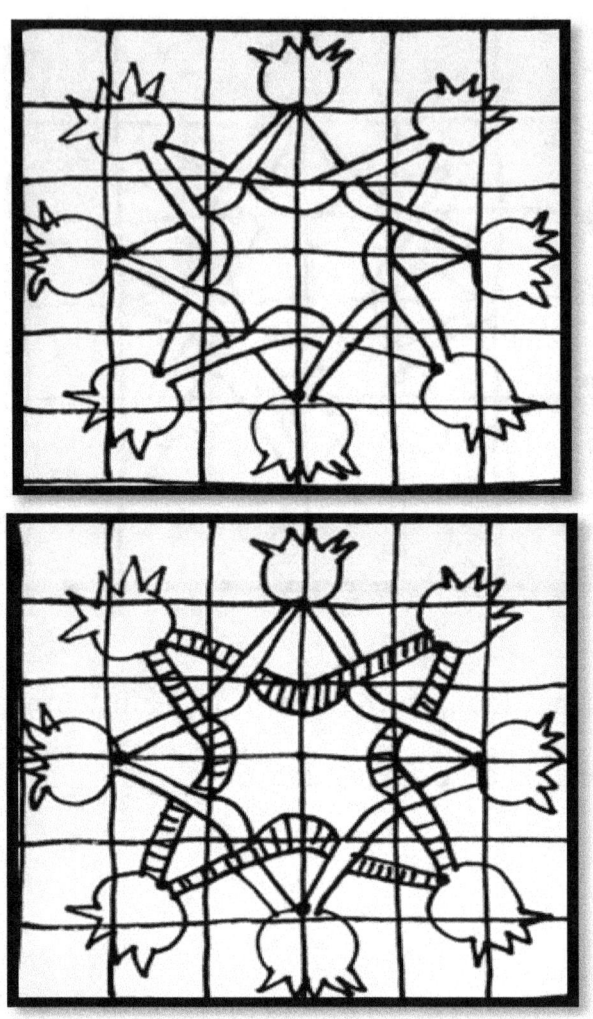

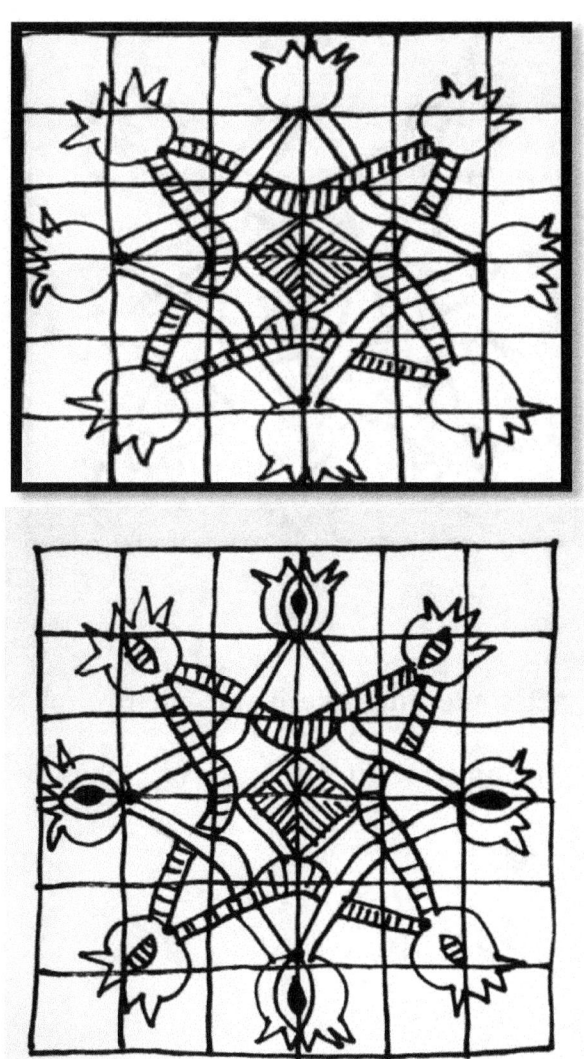

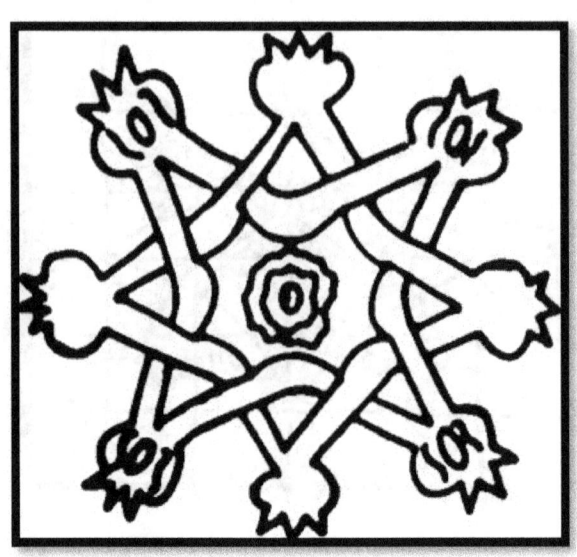

Or you can get something like in the picture on the left. I've erased the grid and I didn't fill the branches with lines. It really looks tangled.

Eke 2

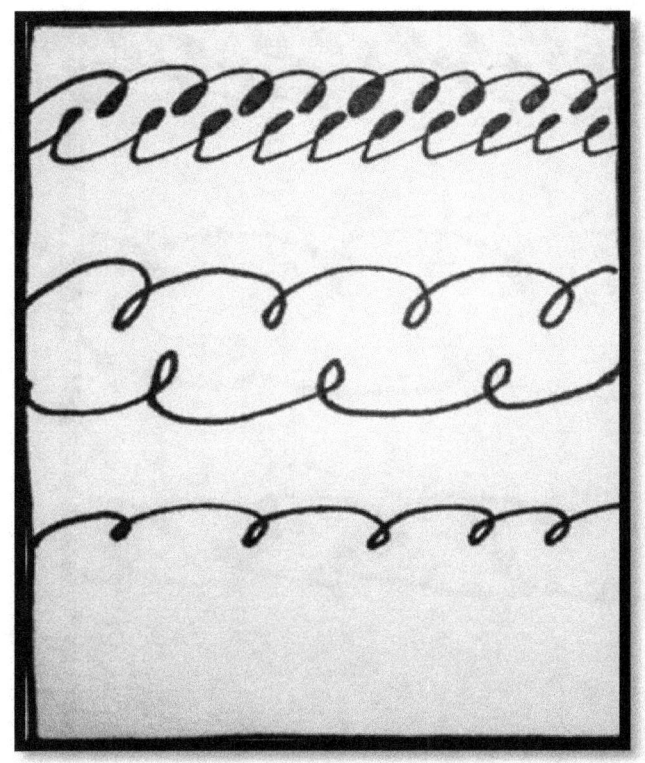

This is a variation of a famous pattern named Eke that begins with a line on which you create loops, which resemble little-written letter e.

I named it Eke 2 as it reminiscences me of something ugly, but I still very much enjoy drawing it.

You should make sure that you create enough space between the loops in the bottom line so that you could draw loops from the top line. Turn the tile and draw the same line as shown on the picture below.

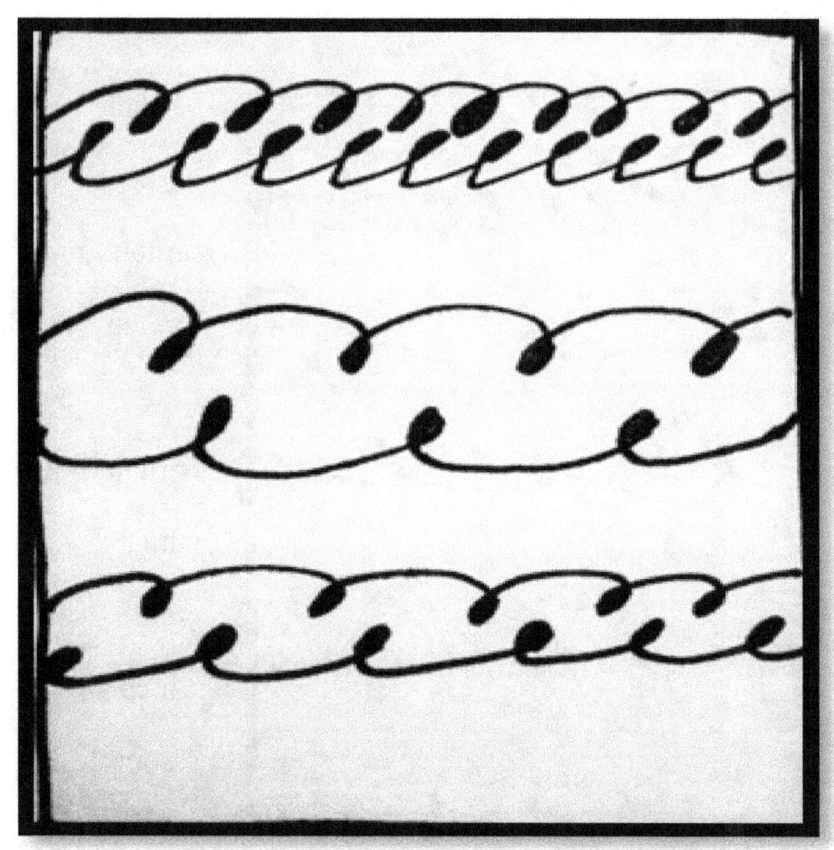

I draw 3 Eke lines on this tile; you can draw as much as you like. Don't forget to fill the loops with a black marker and shade the interior as shown in the picture.

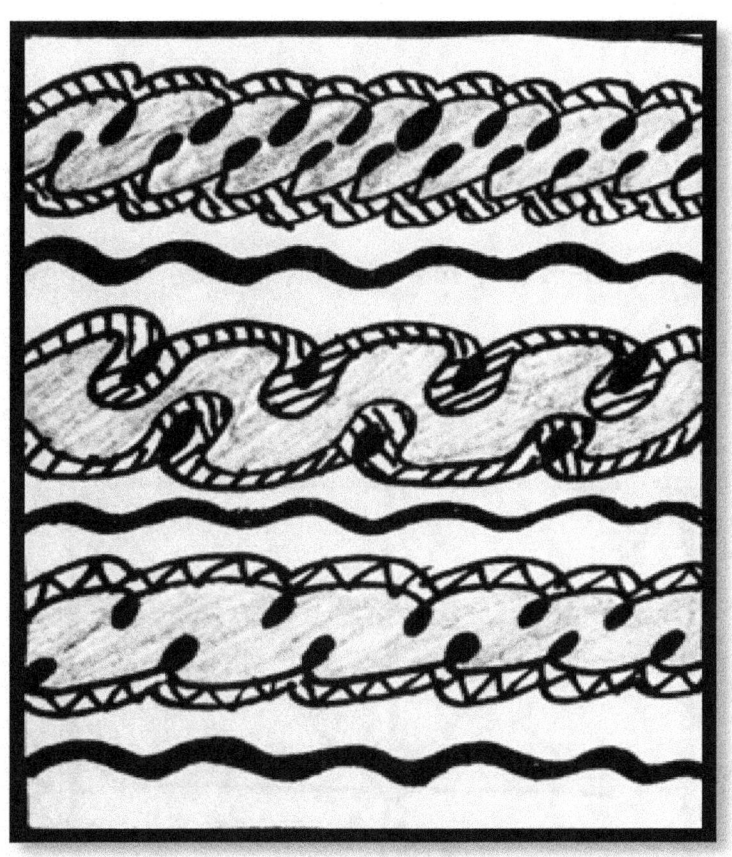

In the end, you might get something that resembles my drawing on the left. As you can see, there are some waves in between.

Sun

As I've already mentioned, I don't like thinking about the names for my Zen drawings, I prefer making them rather than giving them some fancy names. This pattern is inspired with one called Drupe, but it just reminds me of the sun.

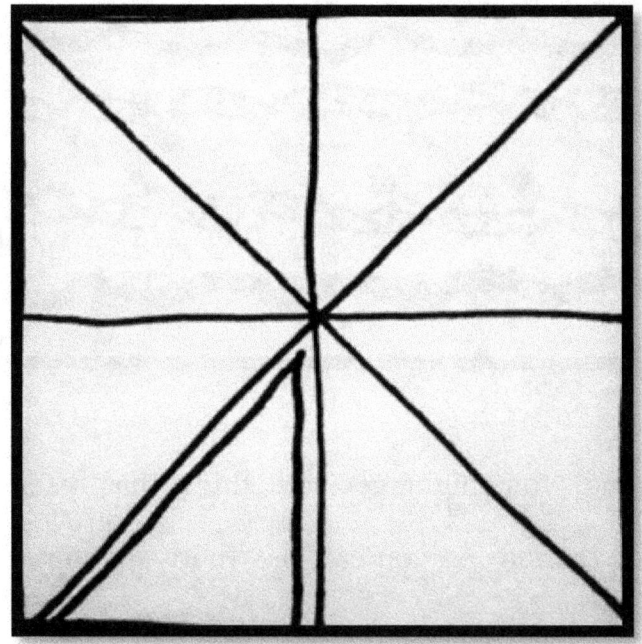

It all starts with four crossed double lines like in the first 2 drawings.

Then, between every two tentacles draw a triangle that follows the lines of the tentacles. For the rest, follow the instructions in the pictures below.

You will come up with a beautiful flower behind the crossed lines and then you can add some patterns to make a drawing more vivid. When you look at it, it looks like it leads you into depth of eternity like in hypnosis. That's why many people call Zen drawings psychedelic art.

It may even seem easy at first sight for you to draw Zen doodles, but your concentration and focus will be well tested once you begin.

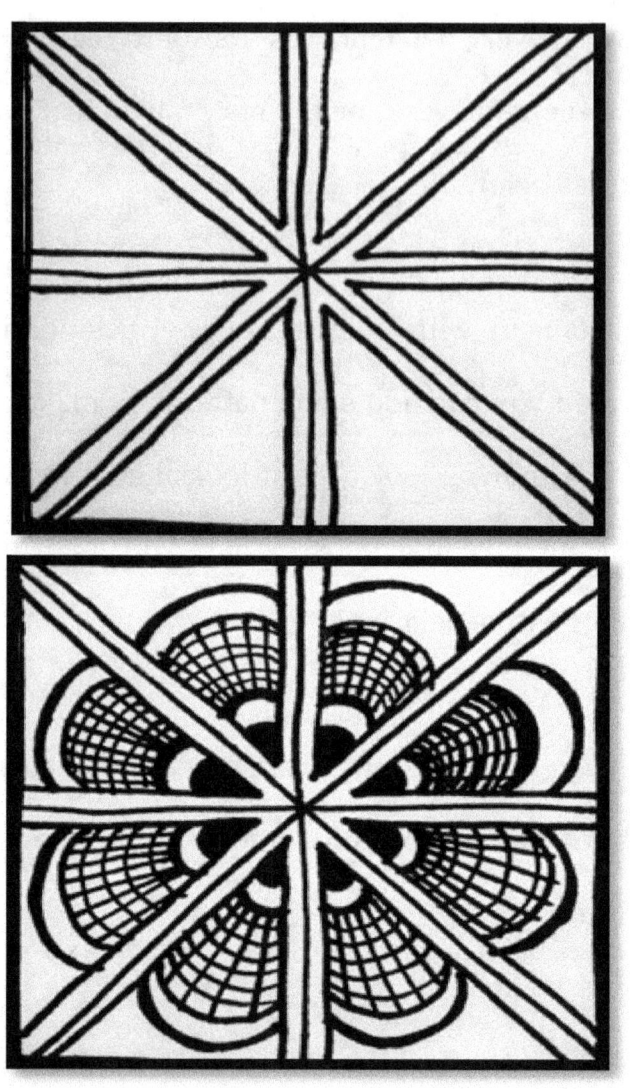

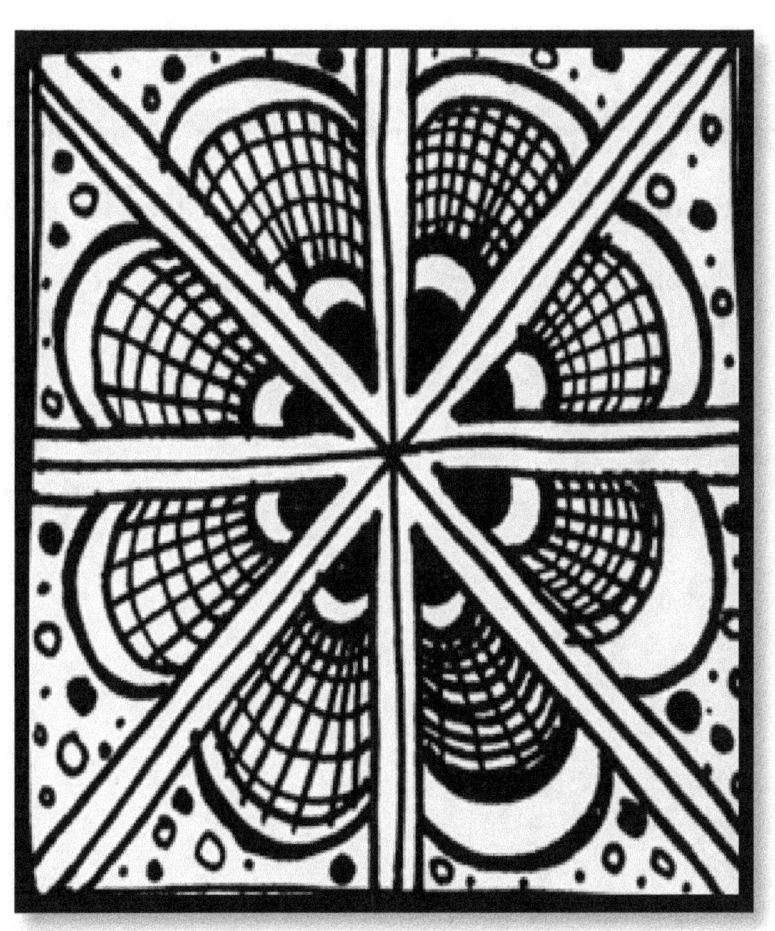

Eyes

There is another option on how to draw Gran, but this drawing reminded me of curious eyes so I called it that way. Follow the pictures below.

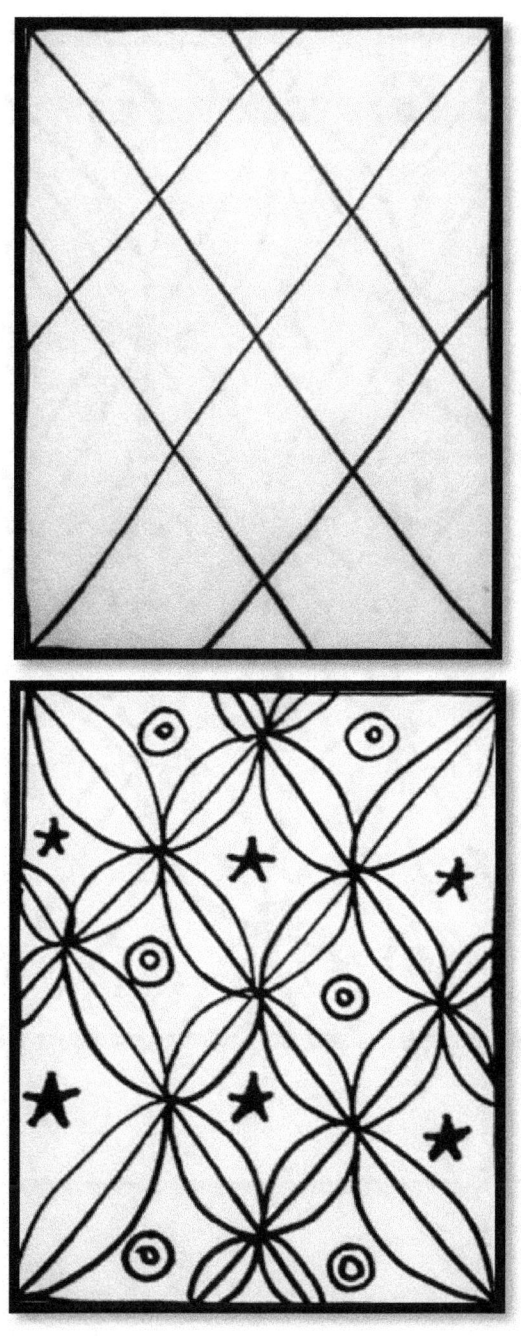

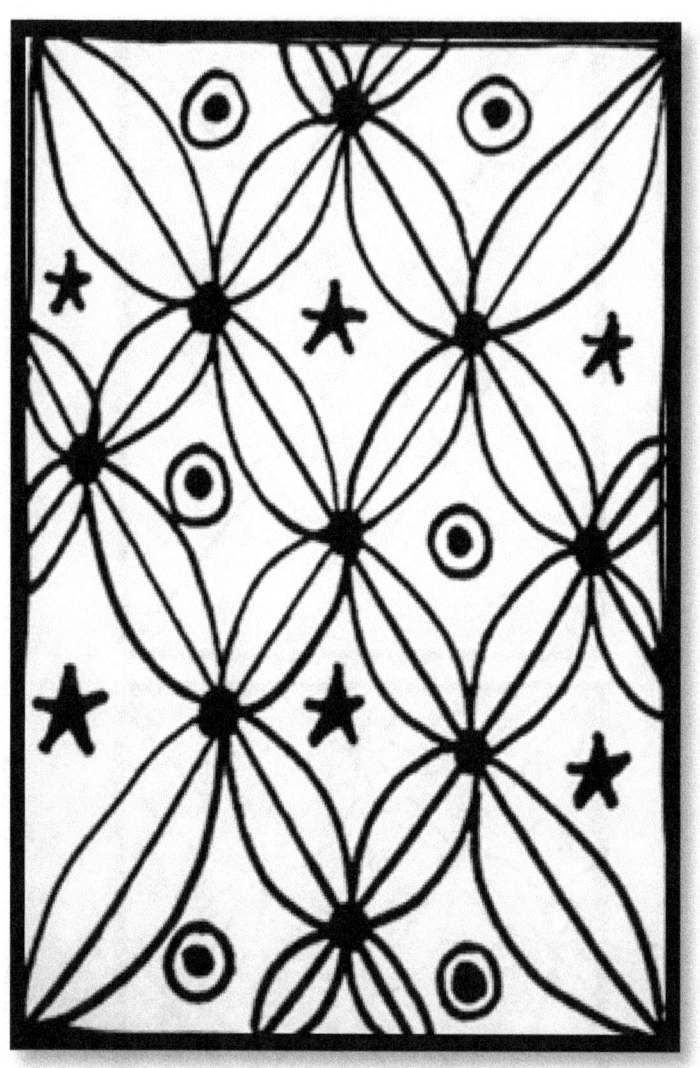

Toto

For this pattern, I got the inspiration on the internet looking at a drawing titled Ozzie. I like to draw and paint geometric figures. Since I was bored with one-point symmetry, I escaped the manner in a way that I have painted triangles and rectangles.

Again, I strongly advise you to use a ruler and a graphite pen at first or you will be making lots of mistakes if you are a beginner. As you can see on the first picture below it all starts with one diagonal line from the upper left corner.

When you draw a rhombus and all those triangles in the gaps, be very careful when you paint with a black or any other color since it gave me a lot of trouble. Who knows, maybe you are better in concentrating.

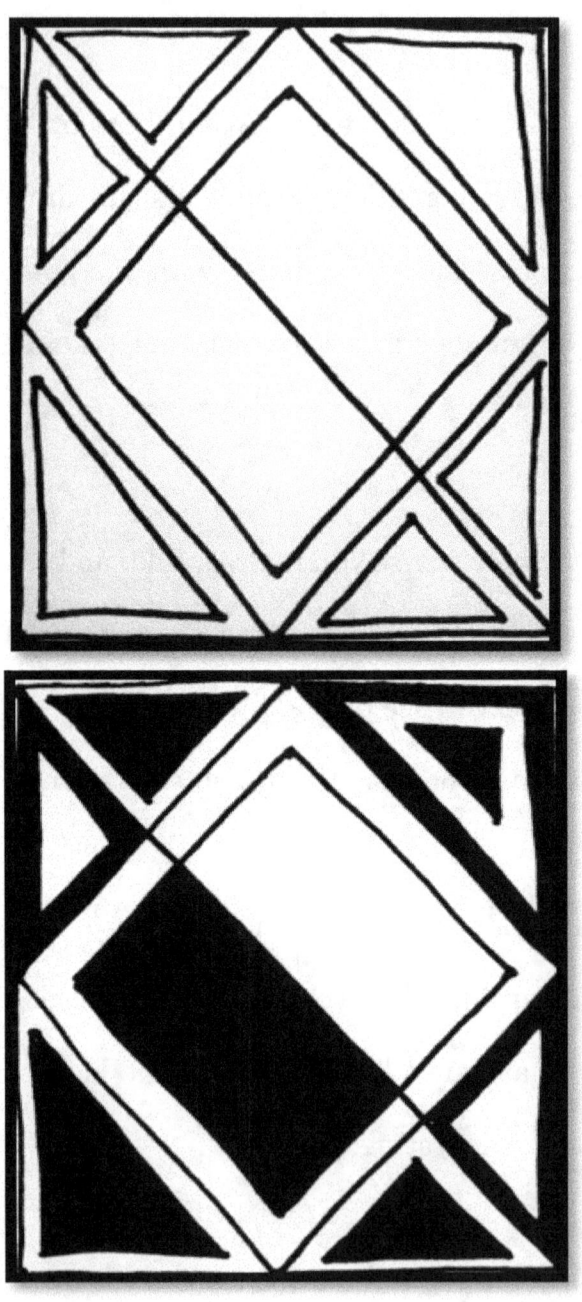

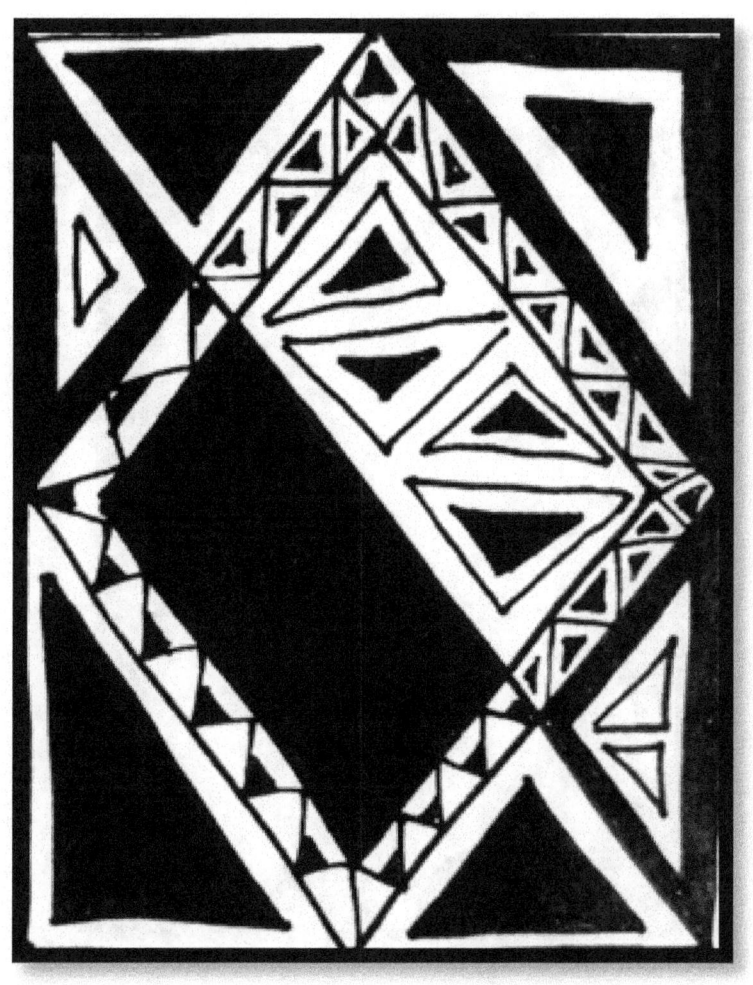

In my personal opinion, it would look nice on your wall.

Faraway

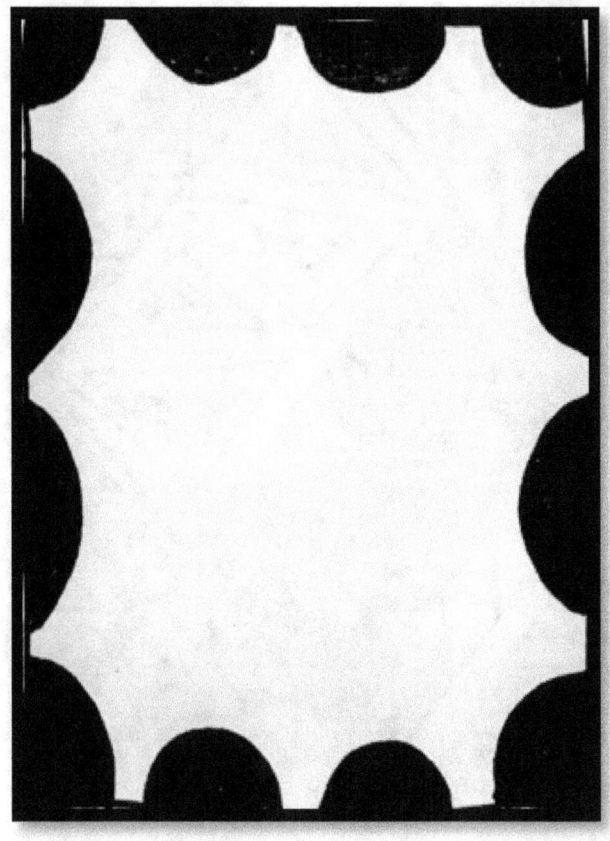

I was inspired to draw **Faraway** when I saw a Zentangle pattern titled Crescent Moon. When I look at this Zen drawing, I feel there is no end of anything. We start by drawing half-moons at the edges of the tile. These half-moons are slightly apart as you can see in the picture on the left. Then we paint its inside with a black marker. After that, you will draw wraps around half-moons.

Then, just follow the lines of the half-moons until you reach the point to have a sort of a "window" in your drawing. After, I just painted some parts with black marker. It's truly a strange and interesting perspective.

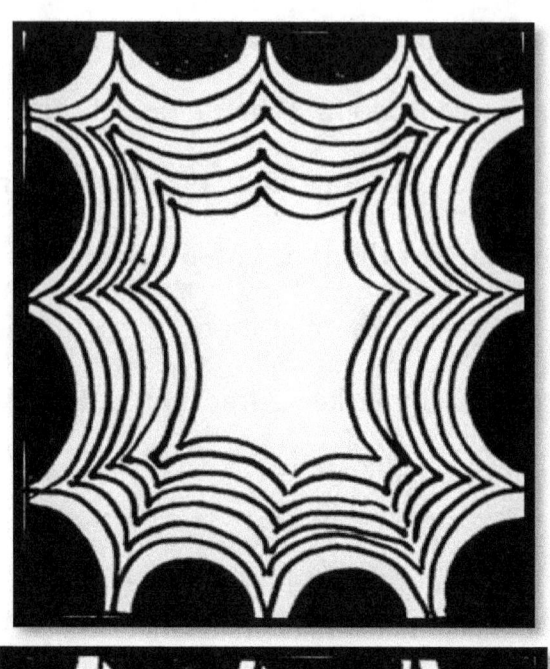

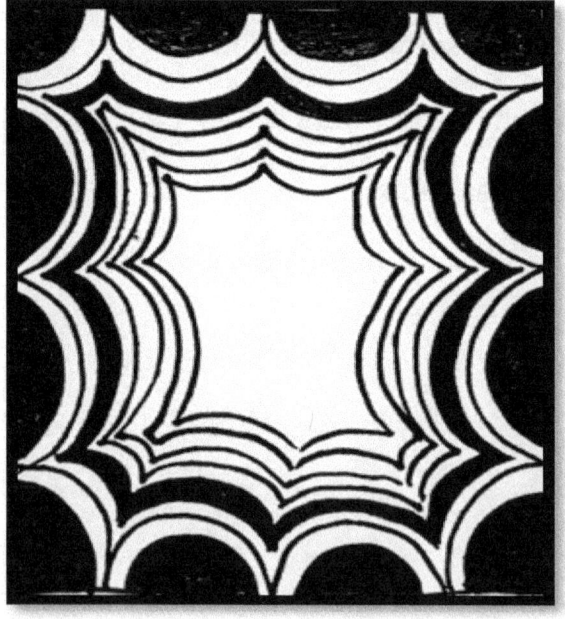

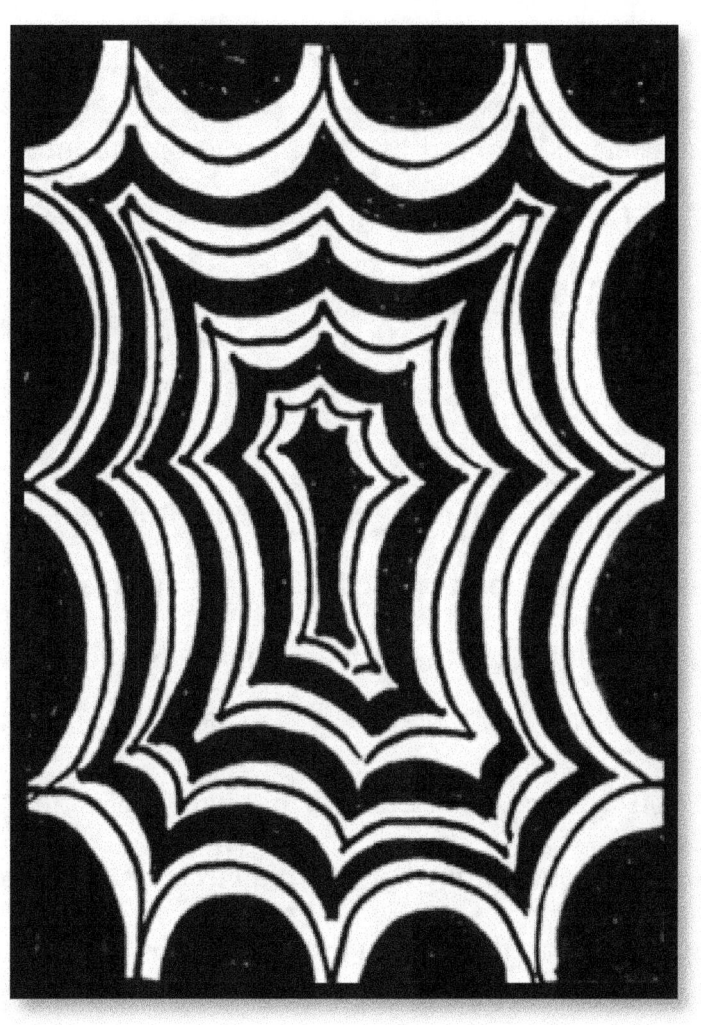

Fifa

This pattern is inspired by one I found on the internet and is called Oof. It reminded me of a football so I named it Fifa. It is not difficult to draw and leaves plenty of space for your creativity.

The only things I can recommend when drawing large inner circles is to use a graphite pencil and try as much as possible to free yours hand. Follow the instructions on the pictures below.

First, you will draw those circles and half-circles on the edge and after you have to draw just 4 big circles in the middle of the tile that overlap those from the edges.

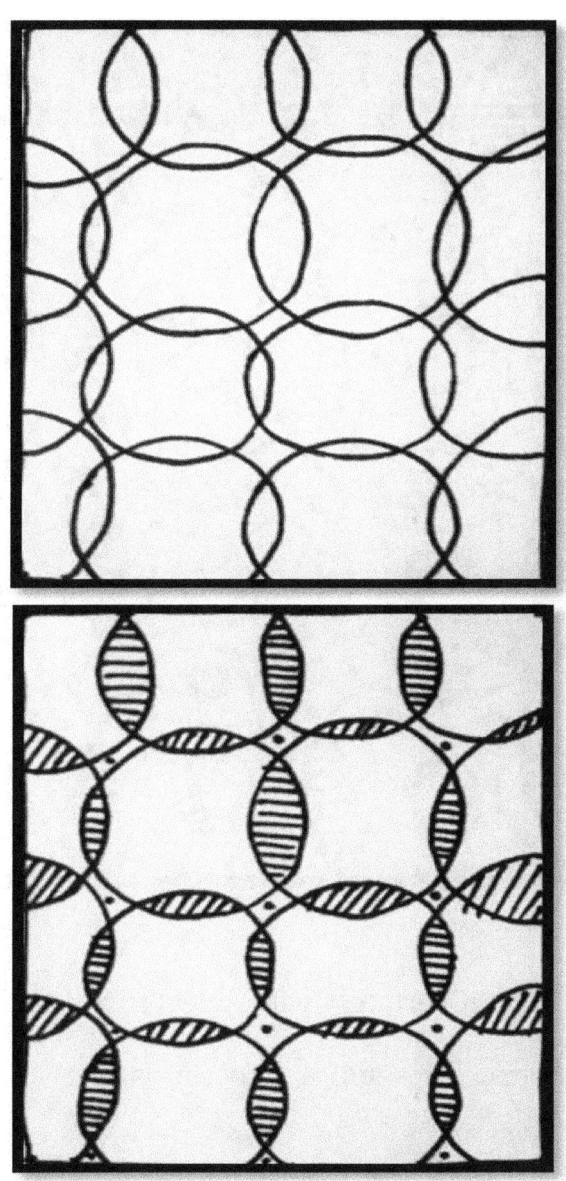

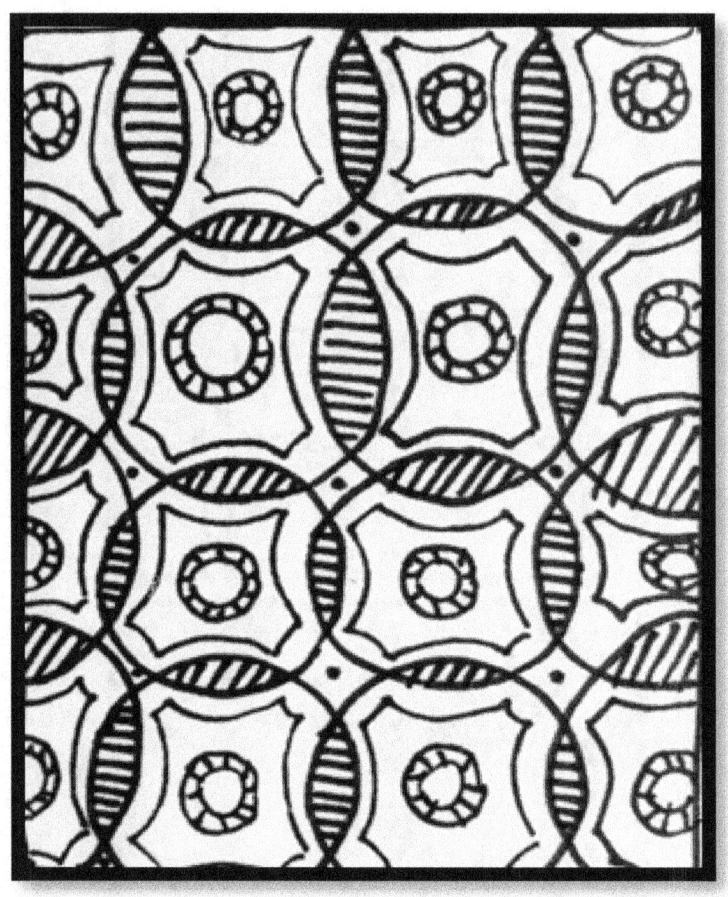

If nothing else, it certainly will appeal to a little boy in your family considering it resembles a soccer ball.

Bucky

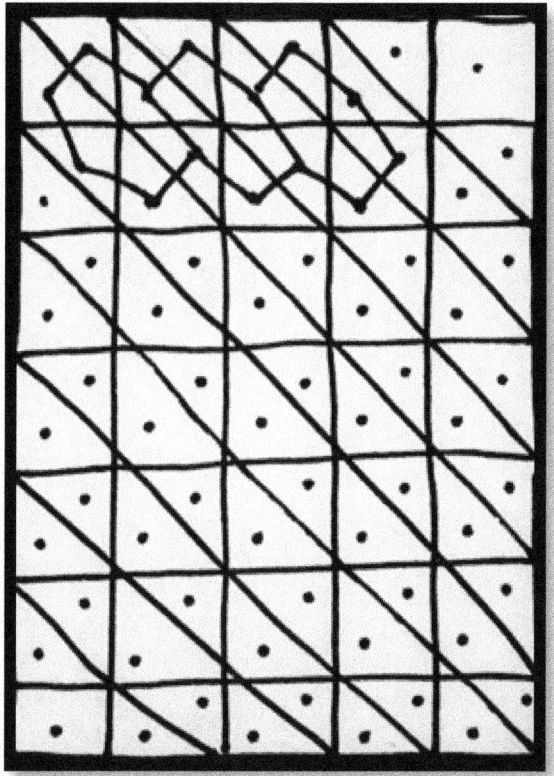

This pattern was inspired by one of the official patterns created by Maria Thomas, called Bucky. To draw this design, you will need a really strong nerve and a lot of patience. First, you should draw a field and then diagonals across it.

The next step is filling figures obtained by connecting the dots. Please note that all the lines are in the opposite direction of the neighboring. This pattern will empty your mind 100% as you it requires your entire attention, but I think it's worth it.

You have two variations on the last pictures below. Choose one, or make your own variation, just be free to express yourself.

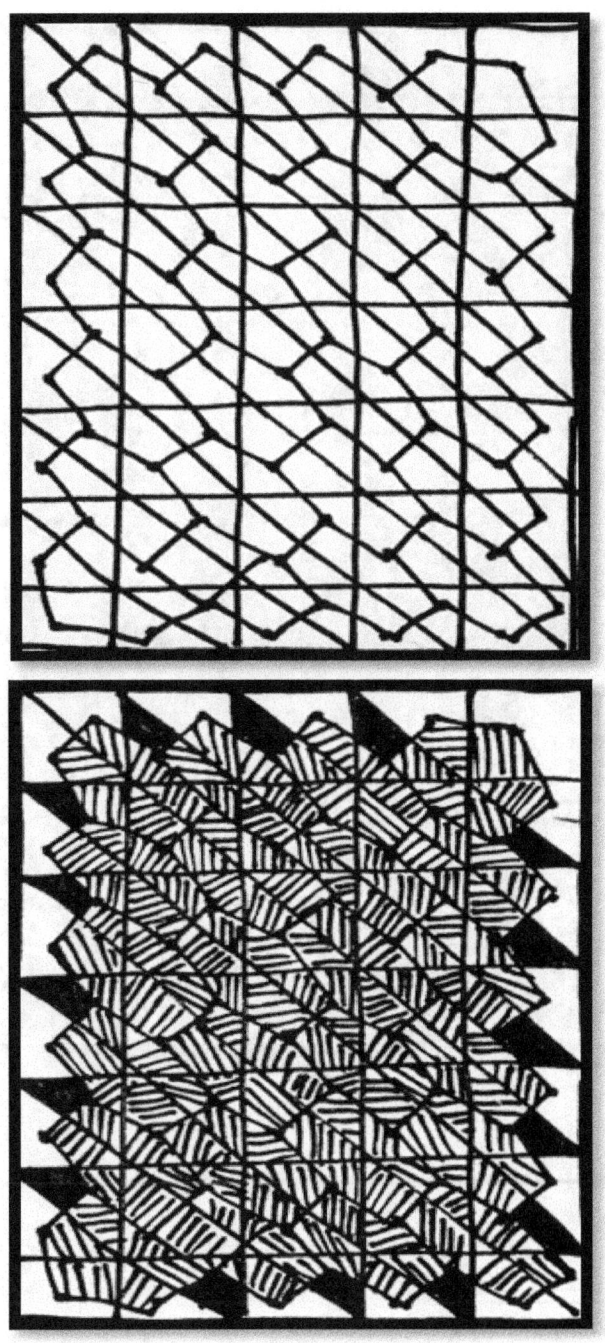

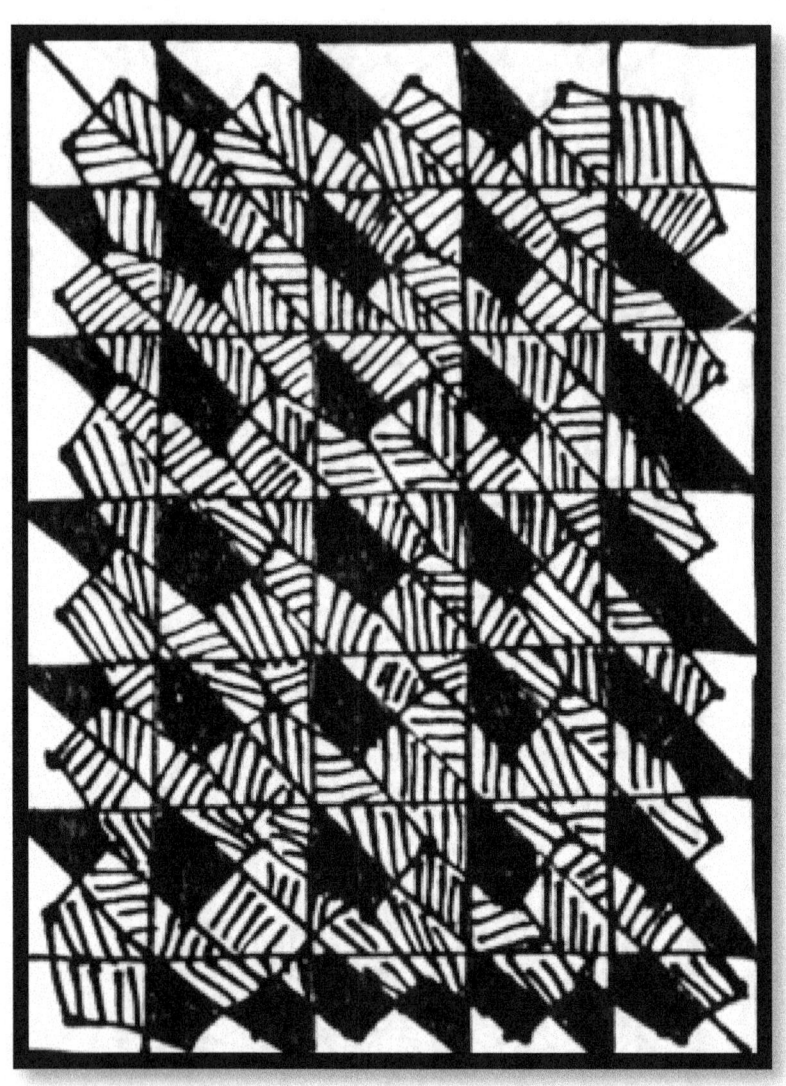

Eye Leaf

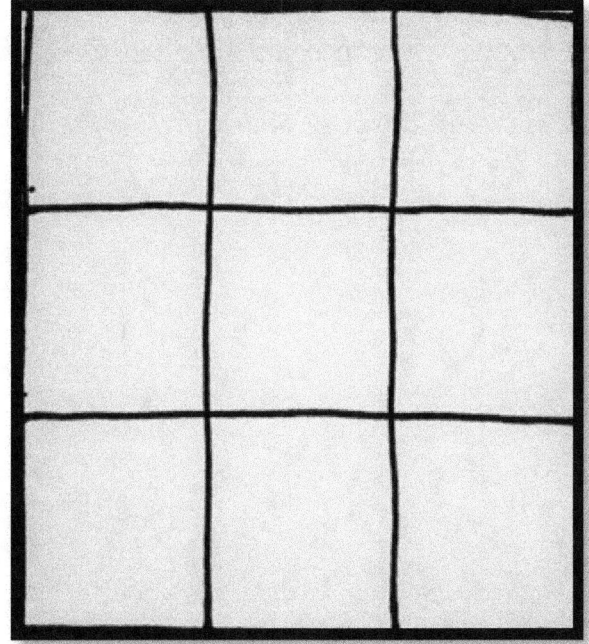

This pattern is also inspired with one of the known patterns. It's not very difficult to draw, and it is interesting. Only take good care of the arrangement of black and white. Of course, in Zen drawing there are no errors, but if you just want to draw Eye Leaf- be careful. Start by drawing a regular field with two vertical and two horizontal lines.

Then head to drawing "leaves" in the fields. When you are finished, paint as shown in the second drawing below. On the third picture below, you can see a finished Eye Leaf pattern. Enjoy, that is the main purpose of any art.

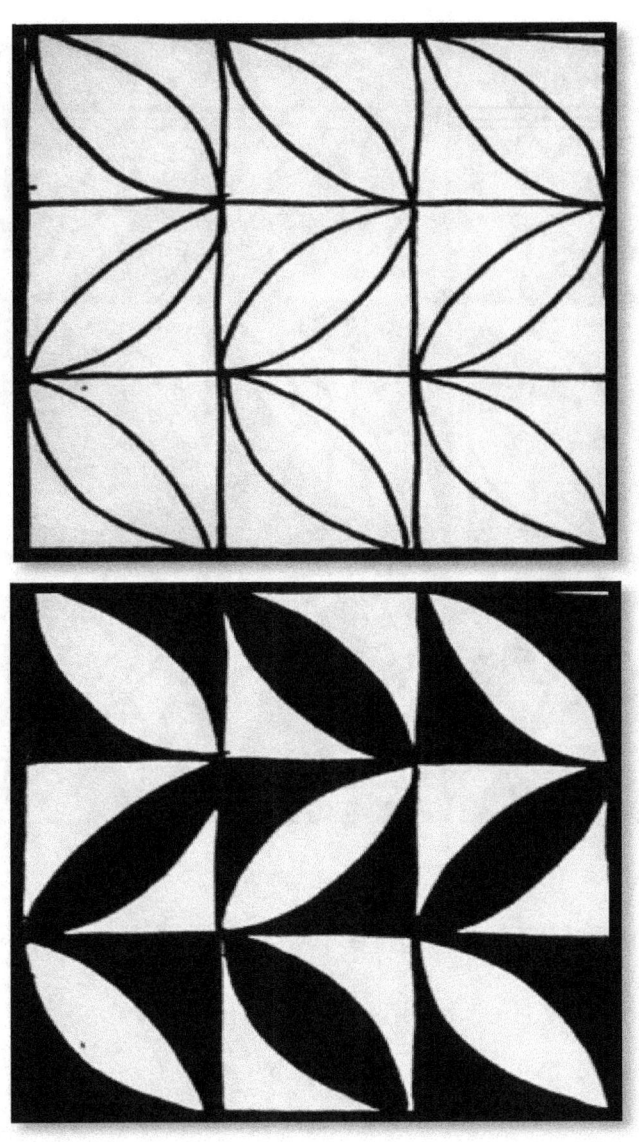

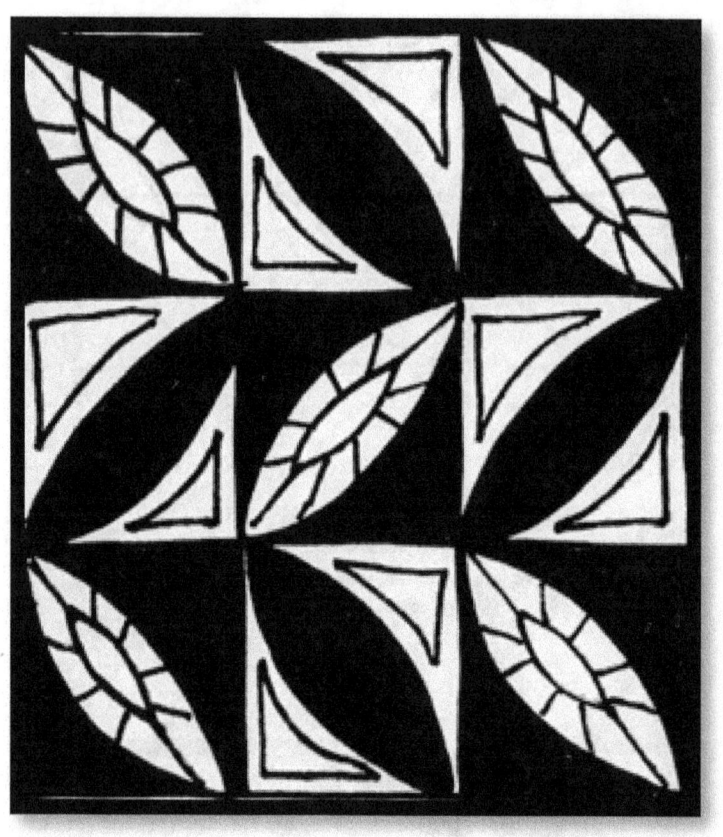

Now, let's move to those patterns you have never seen before, meaning they are inspired entirely by me.

Chapter 4- New Zen doodles

Eyelashes

Let's start with something light at the beginning. Since, in my free time, I am into Zen drawing, while I meditate different patterns comes to me. Eyelashes is one of them; I am not that imaginative when it comes to names of the patterns as I said, but when I think of it, I could as well call it Road. There is nothing complicated, only the lashes should always stand out from the rest of the drawing.

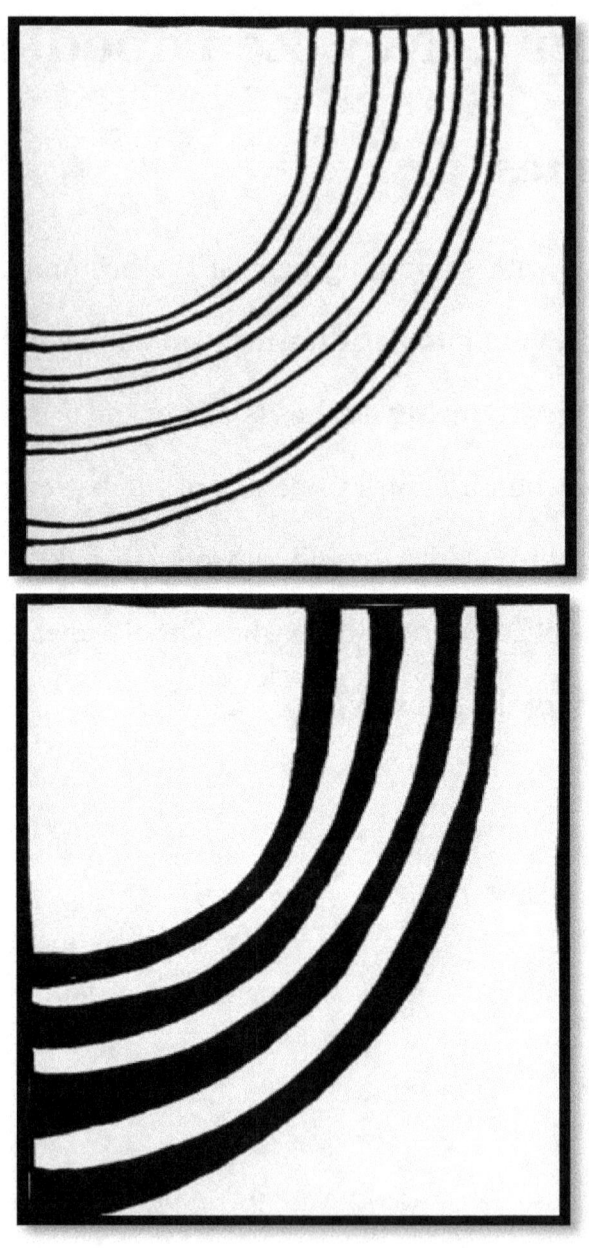

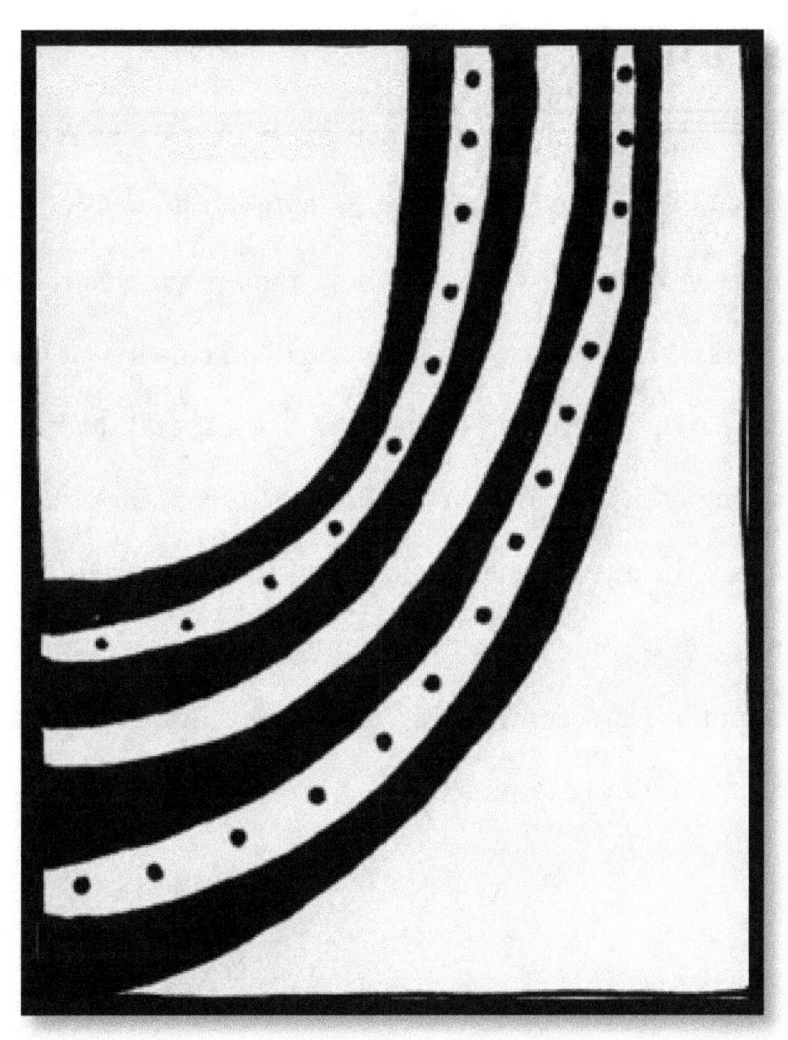

Lost love

This is also one of the new Zen art patterns inspired with basic shapes such as circles, dots and curved lines. I named it lost love as it starts with something that resembles the face with tears. When I started to draw, I had no clue how it will all come up. In this case, I first draw eyes and tears, and everything else just came in the process of creating. I made a mistake as I forget about the nose, but then I figured out it is better this way. So, I came to one more conclusion, and that is you shouldn't erase mistakes- they make drawings unique. After that, you can examine them.

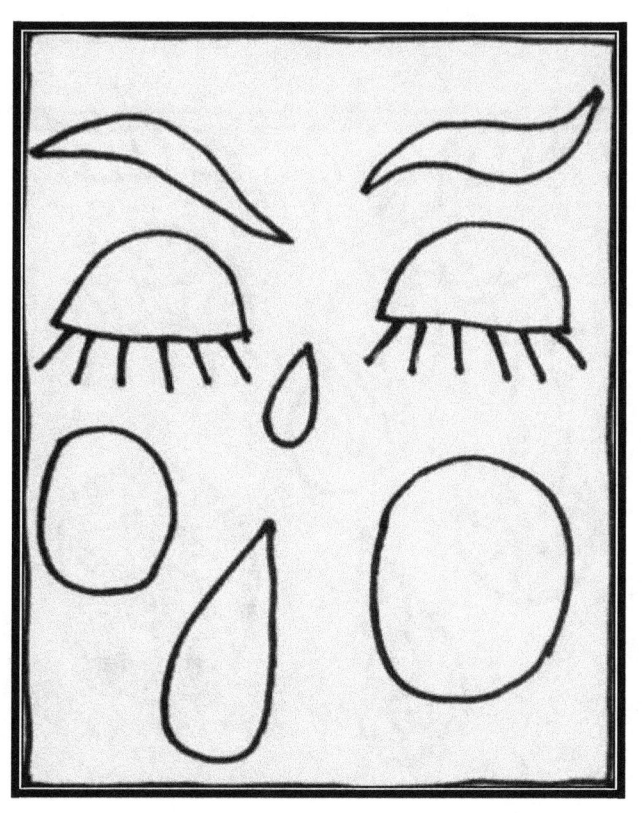

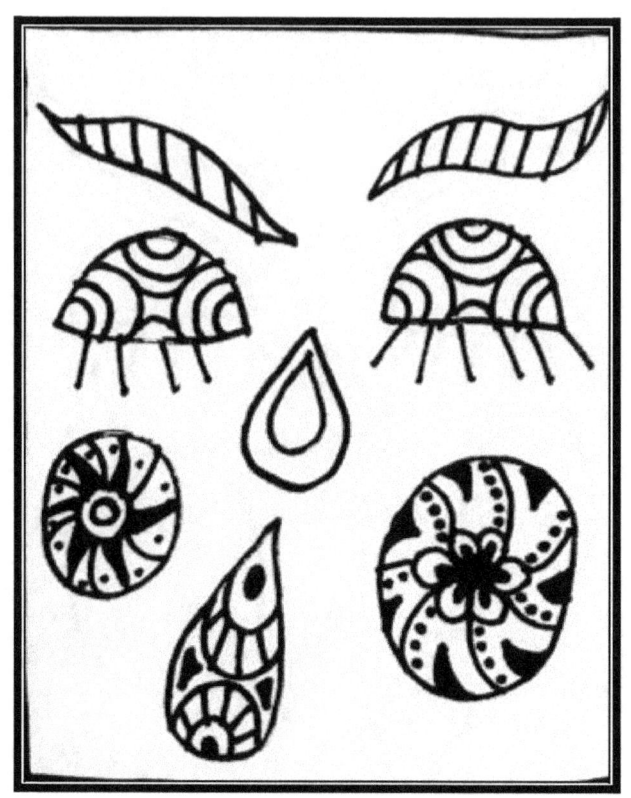

Just follow the pattern on the pictures below and you`ll get something like two turtles (the eyes) in wonderland of Zen art. What was supposed to be the eyebrows, now looks like foliage that protects small "turtles" from the sun. That's the beauty and thrill about Zen drawing: you never know what you'll get when you finish drawing.

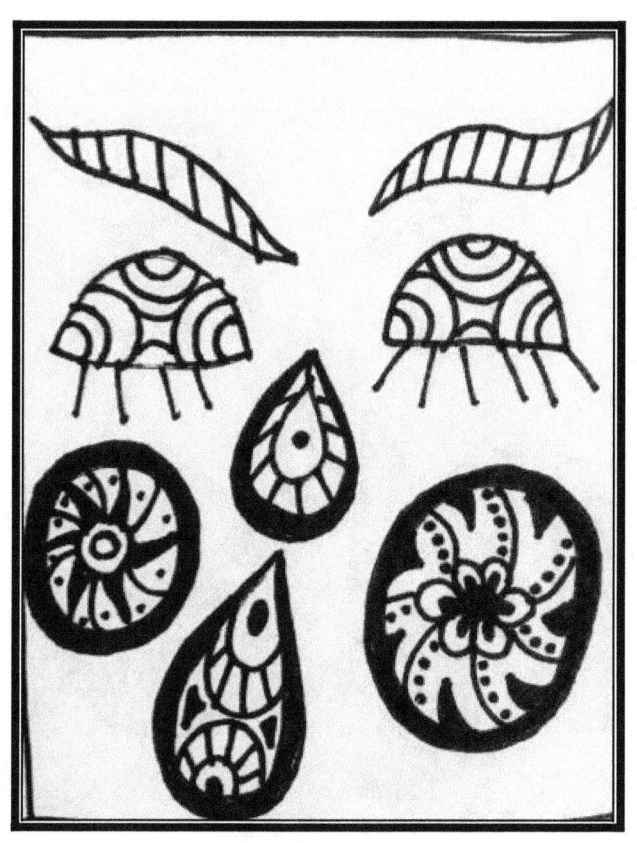

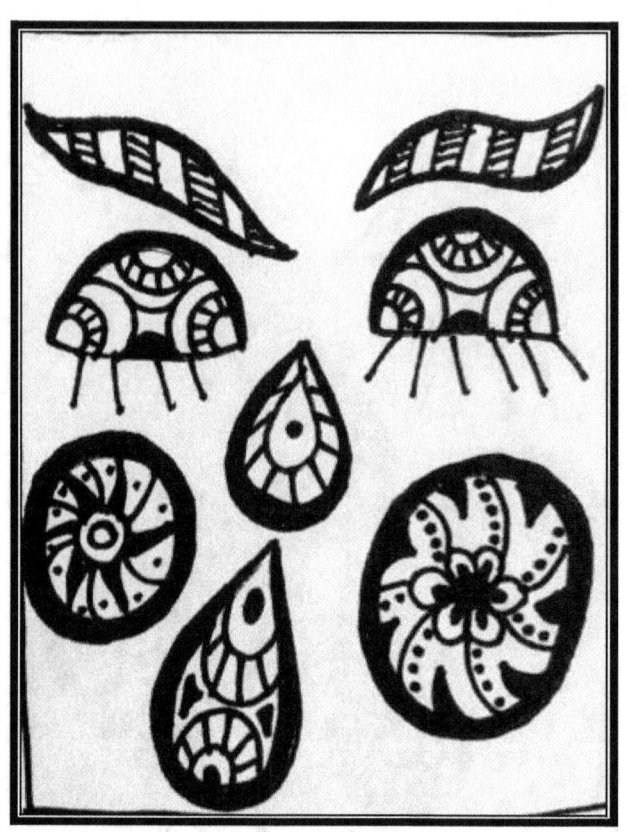

At the end, I`ve added circles and dots to fill out my Zen drawing.

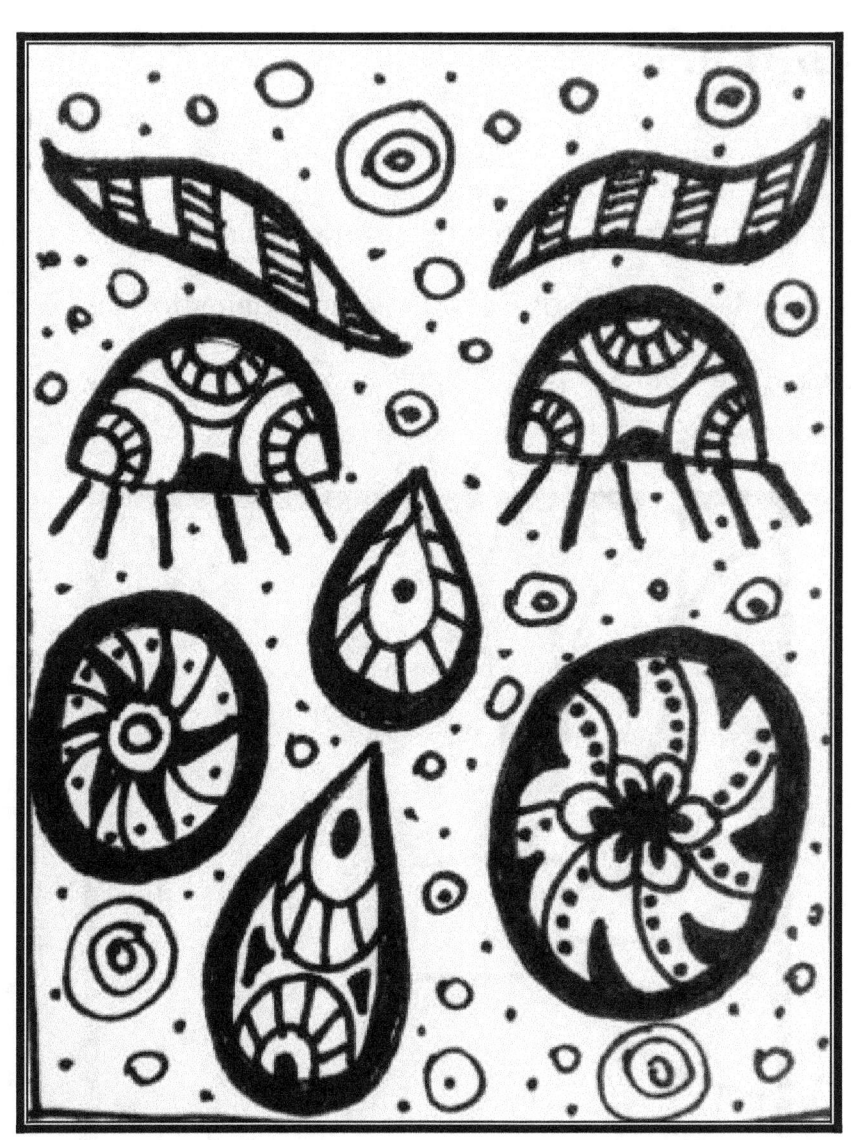

Sunflower

The name speaks for itself, it's the sunflower the way I see it. Just add petals as there is no more available space on the tile, but there is a lot of space for your imagination inside the petals. I have put a small rectangle as a pestle.

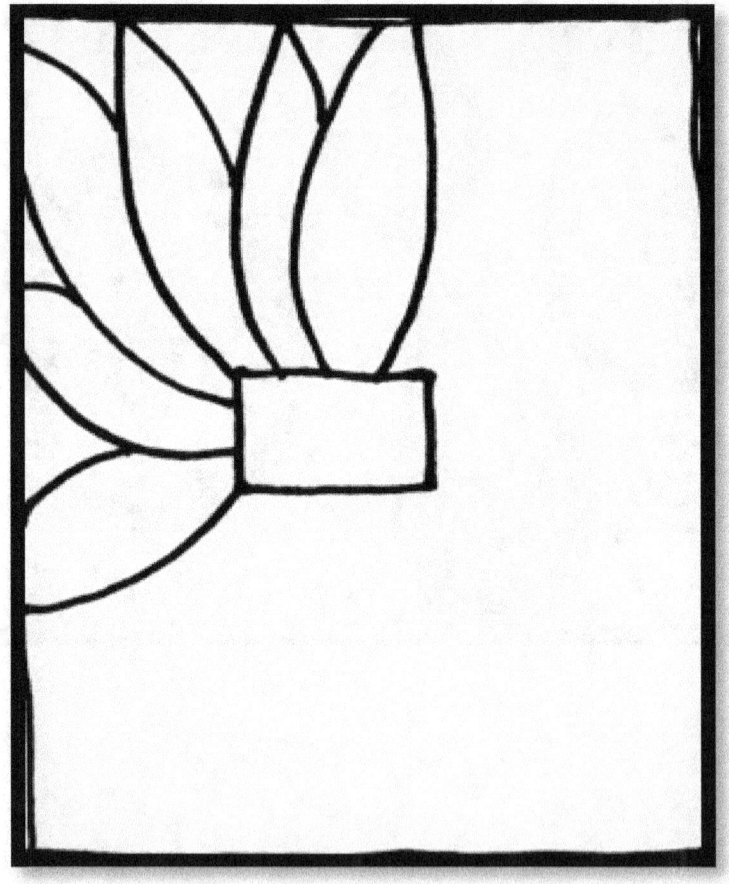

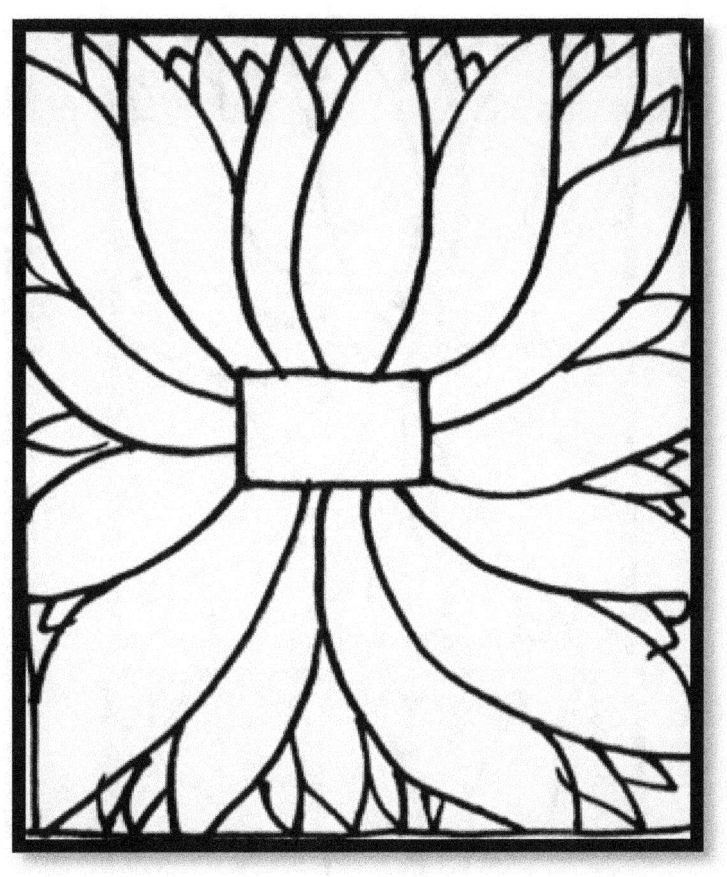

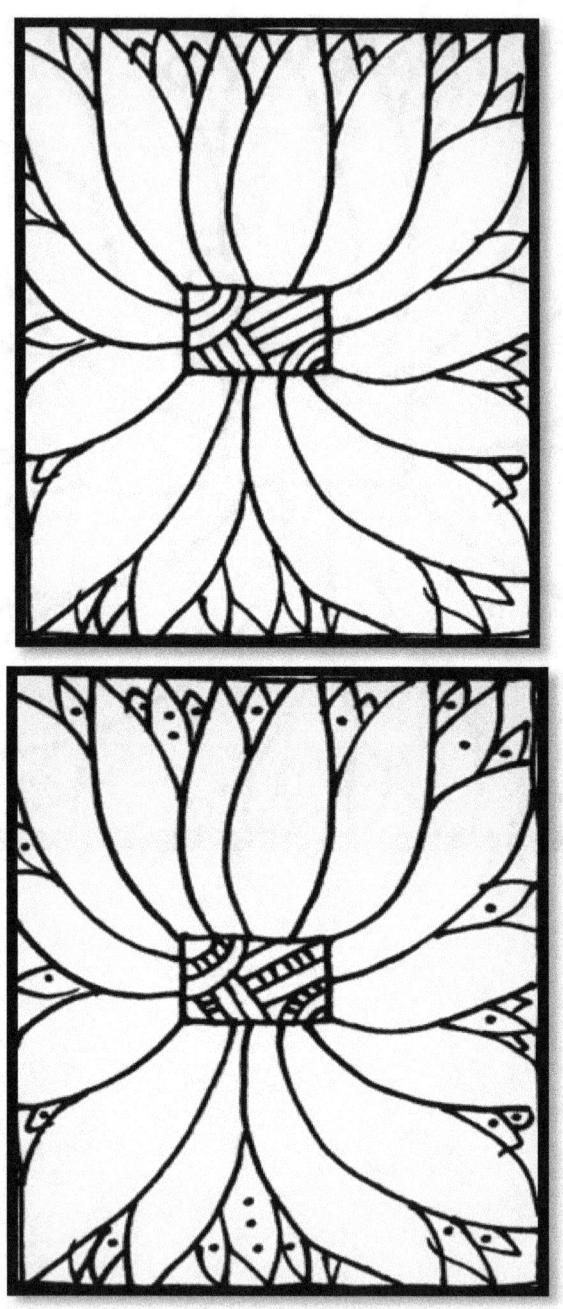

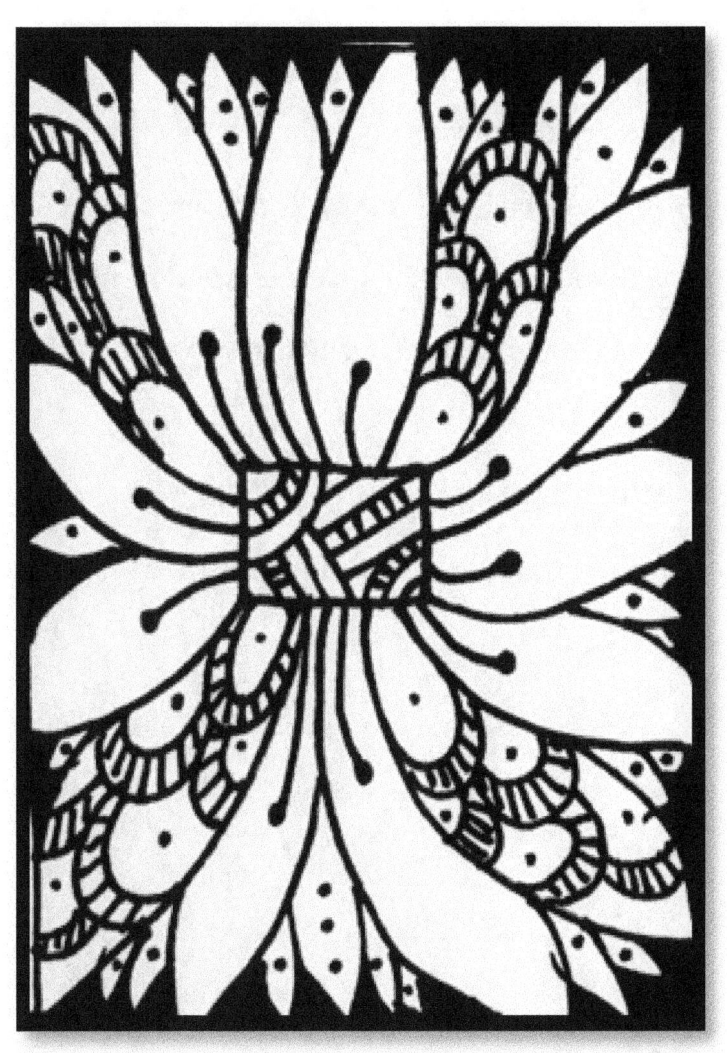

Angry Face

I simply started drawing and then I saw something that looks like an angry face so I named it that way. As you can see from the pictures, I used what I have learned from some other patterns like a **Chess Board** or a **Spotty Dotty** on the right.

It's just the way it goes, you learn different patterns and then you use them in your own drawings to create something unique.

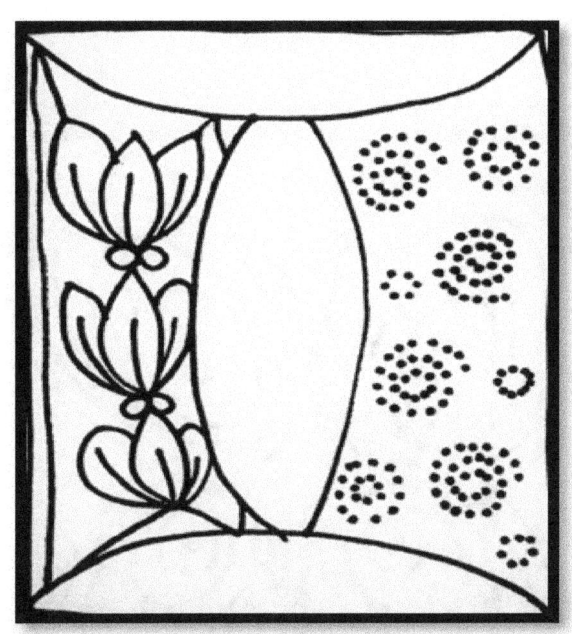

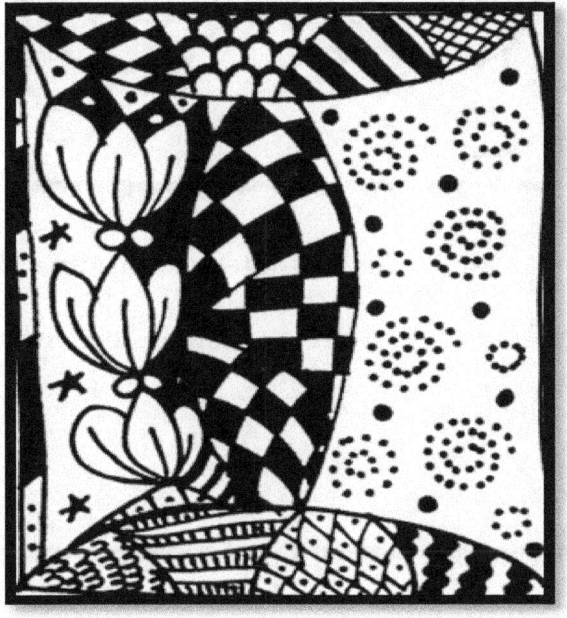

Sneaky

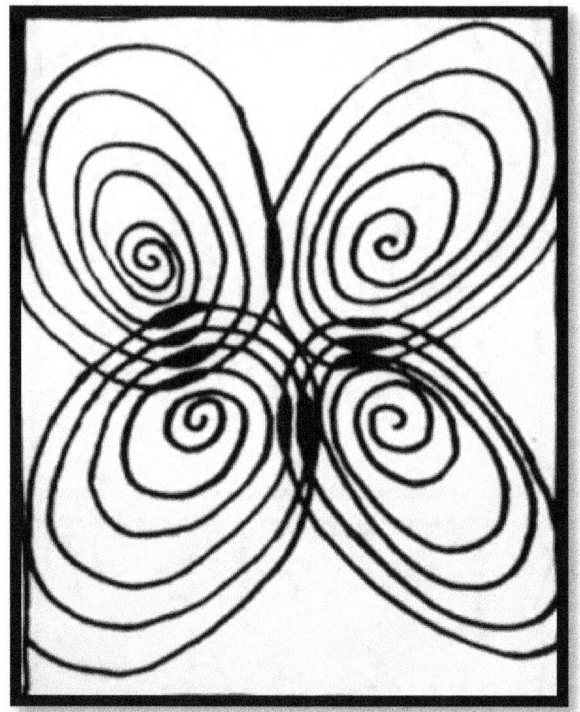

I started to draw spirals that intersect in some places, and it seemed like fun. It reminds of a snail shell or a butterfly-depends on who is watching.

Then, I just made eyes with a black marker and they were becoming bigger and bigger, so I've got Sneaky. It reminds me of a thief.

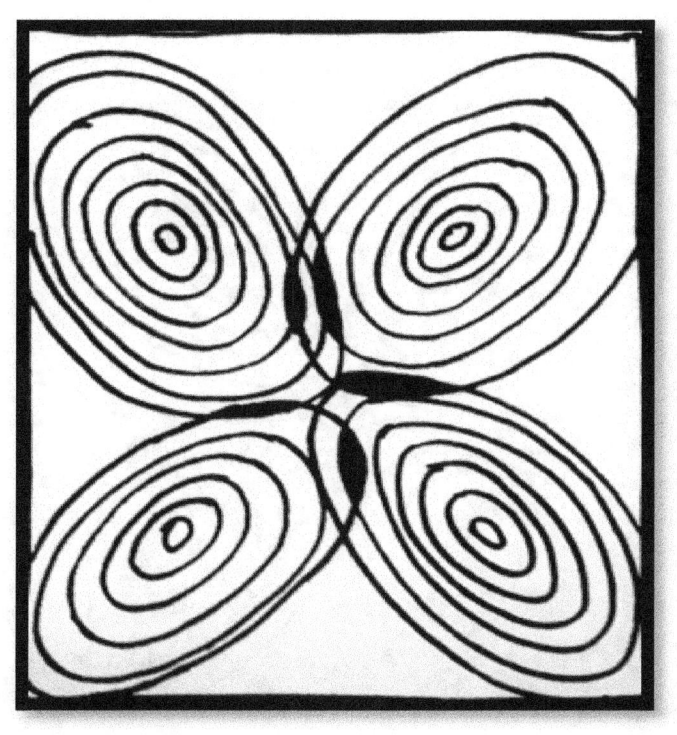

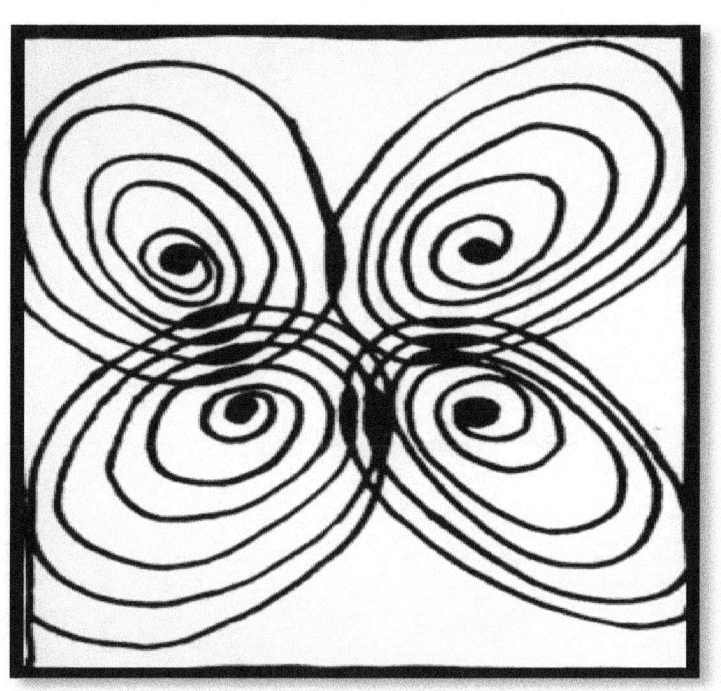

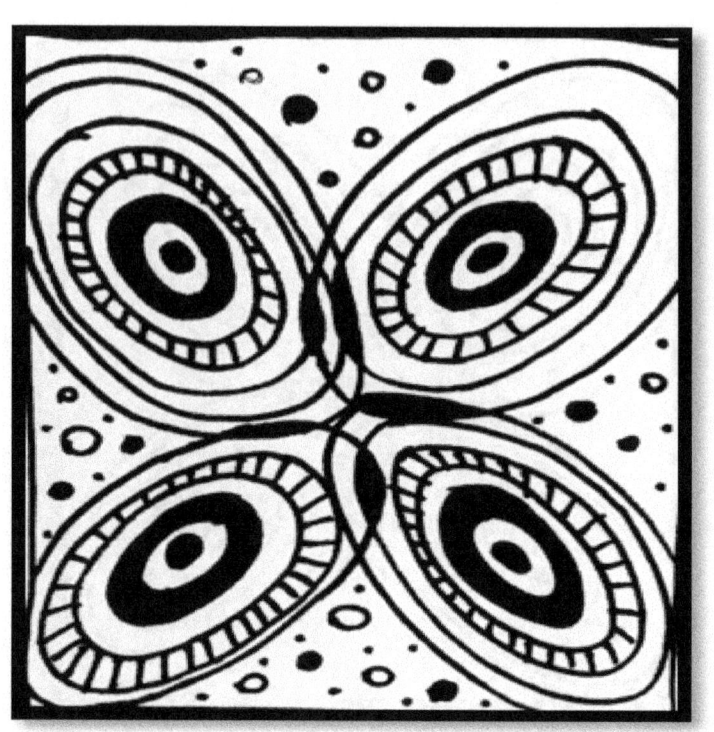

Palm

Now, let's draw something a bit complicated and truly psychedelic. It is a palm so I named this pattern that way. You simply cannot title it differently. You can use your palm to draw a true Zen art filled with various forms and shapes. First, you will replicate your hand on the tile and draw lines to divide the palm in several parts, so that you have more playgrounds.

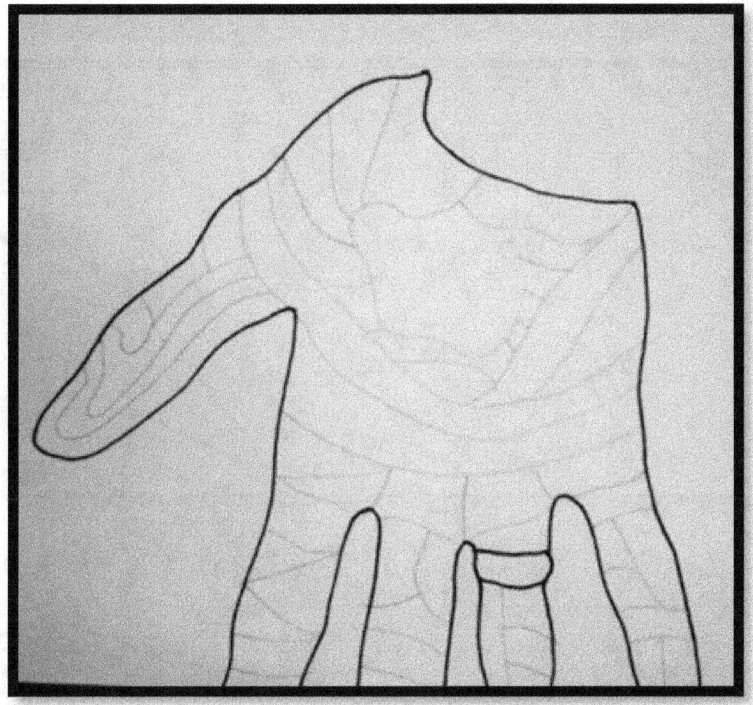

Watch carefully how the lines go; as you can see there is a little puddle in the middle of the Palm. After you have finished drawing with a lead pen, bold the edges of the palm and all the lines inside with a marker.

You can start filling the palm with various forms and drawings from the edge of the thumb as shown on the second picture below.

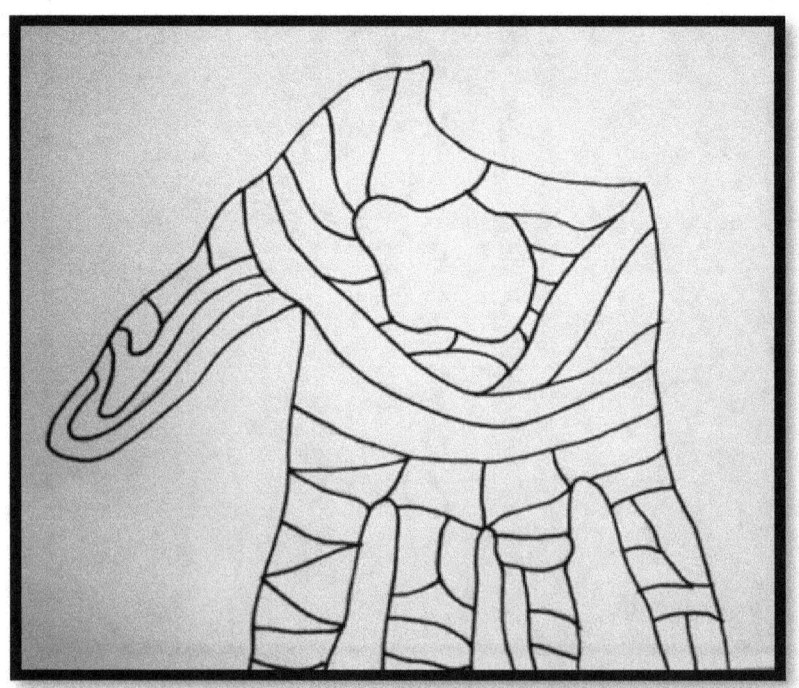

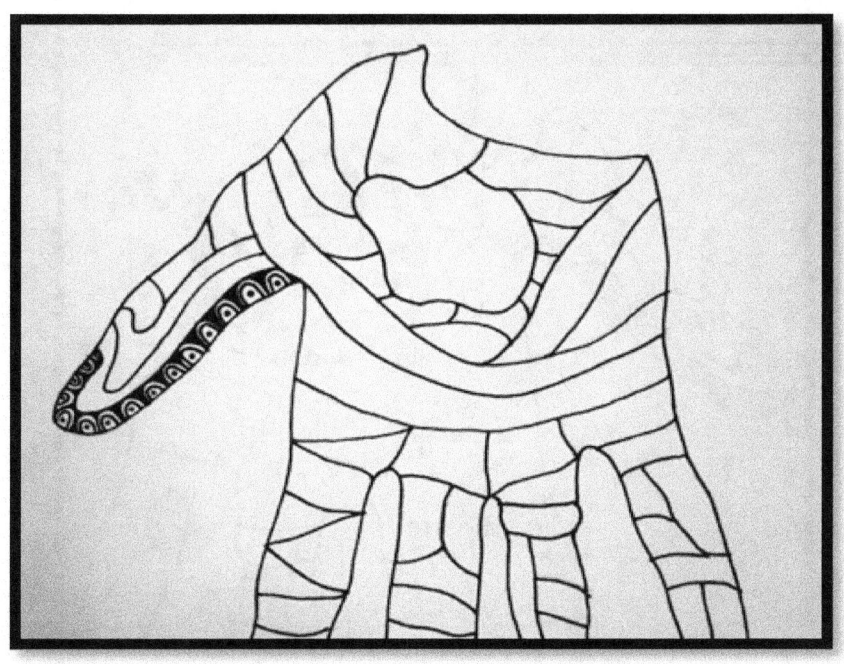

After that, all you can do is to follow the pictures below if you wish to draw the identical Zen doodle as mine. If not, the drawings from below can give you an inspiration for your own "fillings".

The pictures are pretty large, so I think you won't have troubles following the patterns. But, you will need a lot of time to finish this one.

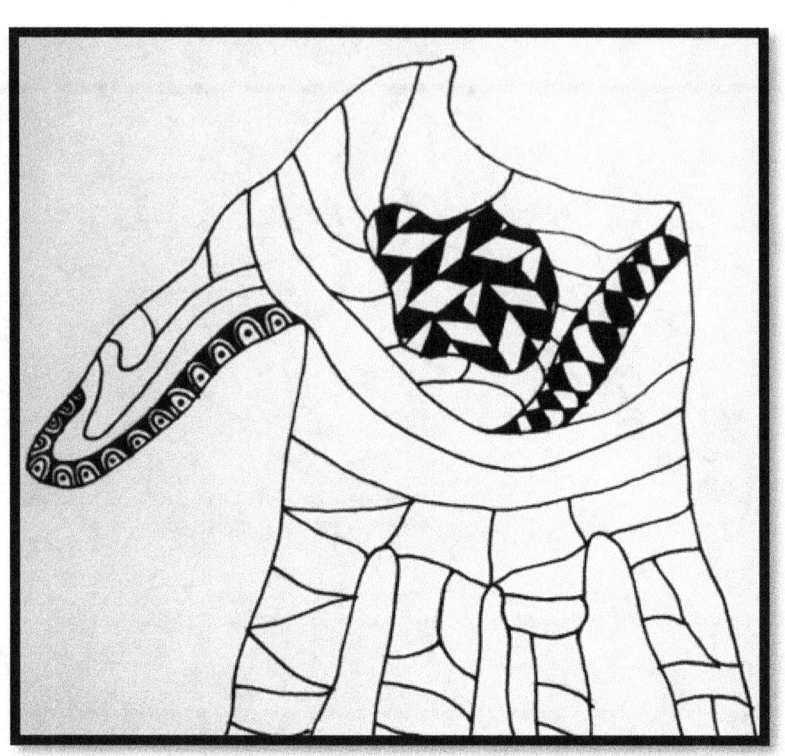

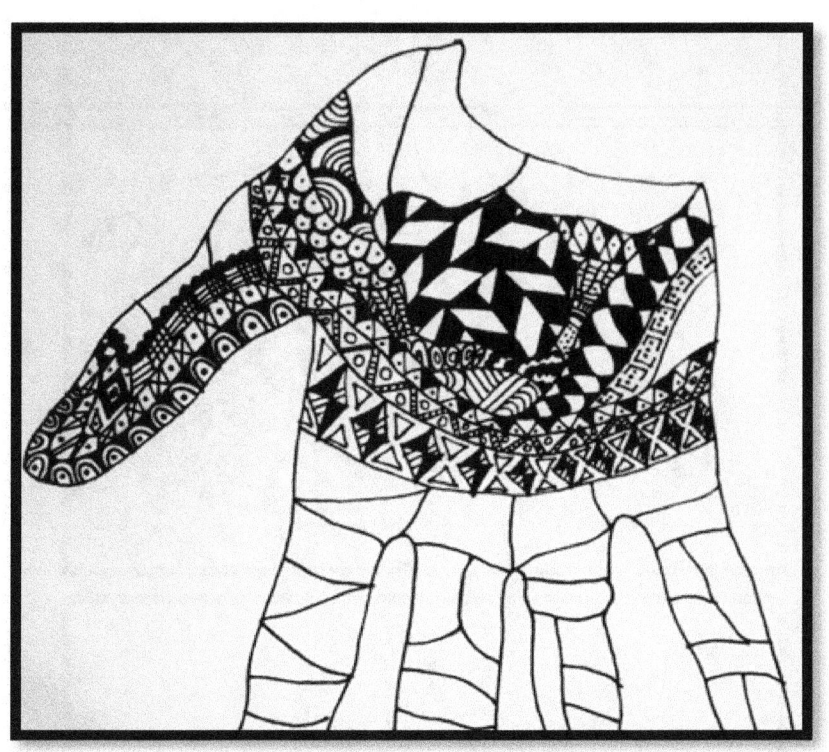

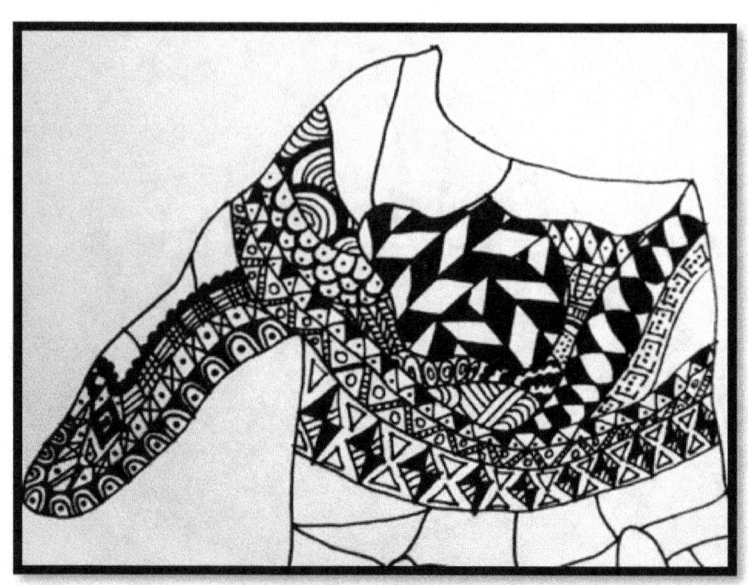

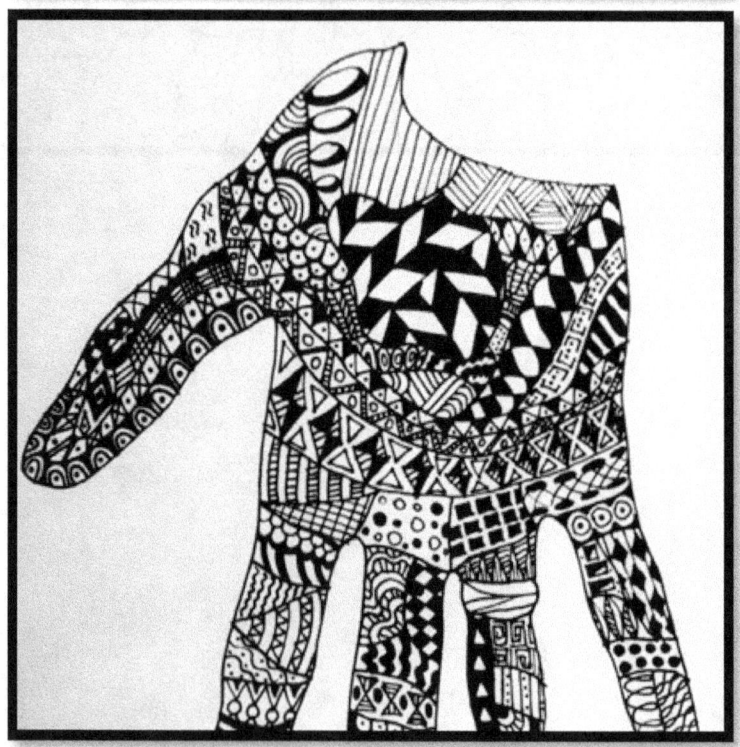

In the end, I've prepared for you **<u>My Heart</u>**. I called it this way since it's really is my heart. I had the intention to draw a pure red heart, but the black marker just tempted me all the time, so I draw a red and black heart. We can all learn a lot about ourselves from our Zen drawings. You can draw your heart to see what's really in there.

First, I pulled 2 crossed lines so I could orient while drawing a heart. The rest is best explained in the pictures.

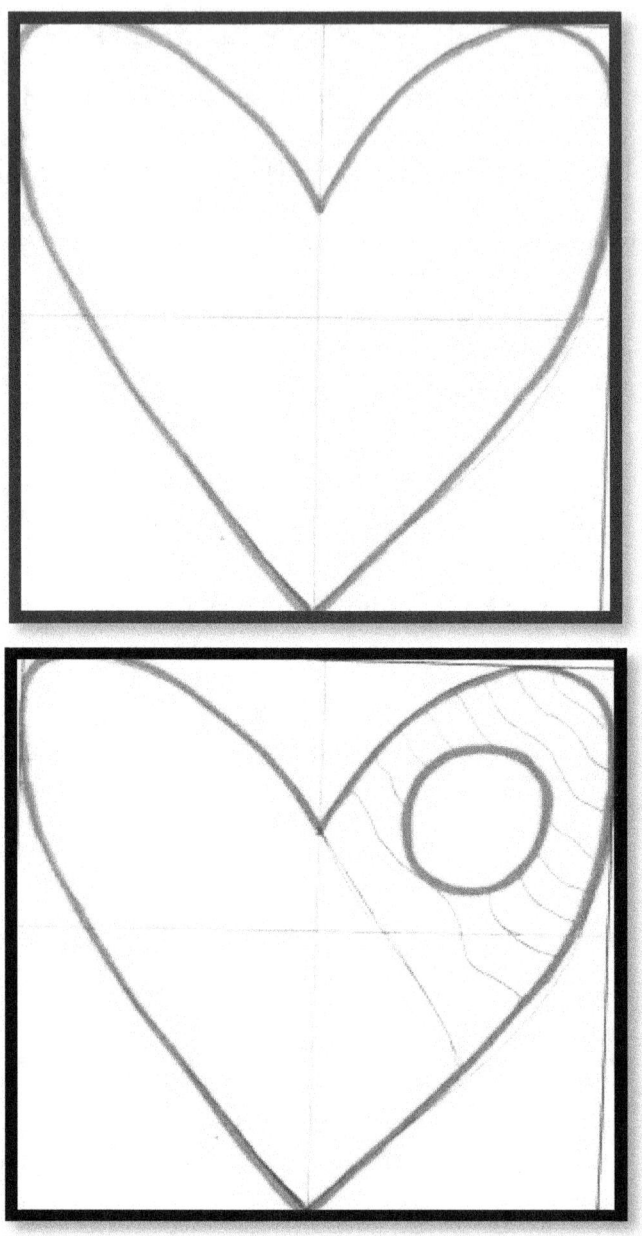

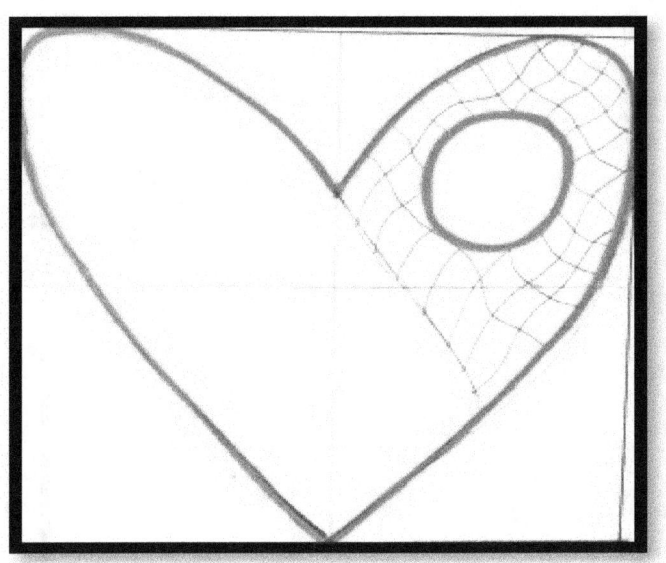

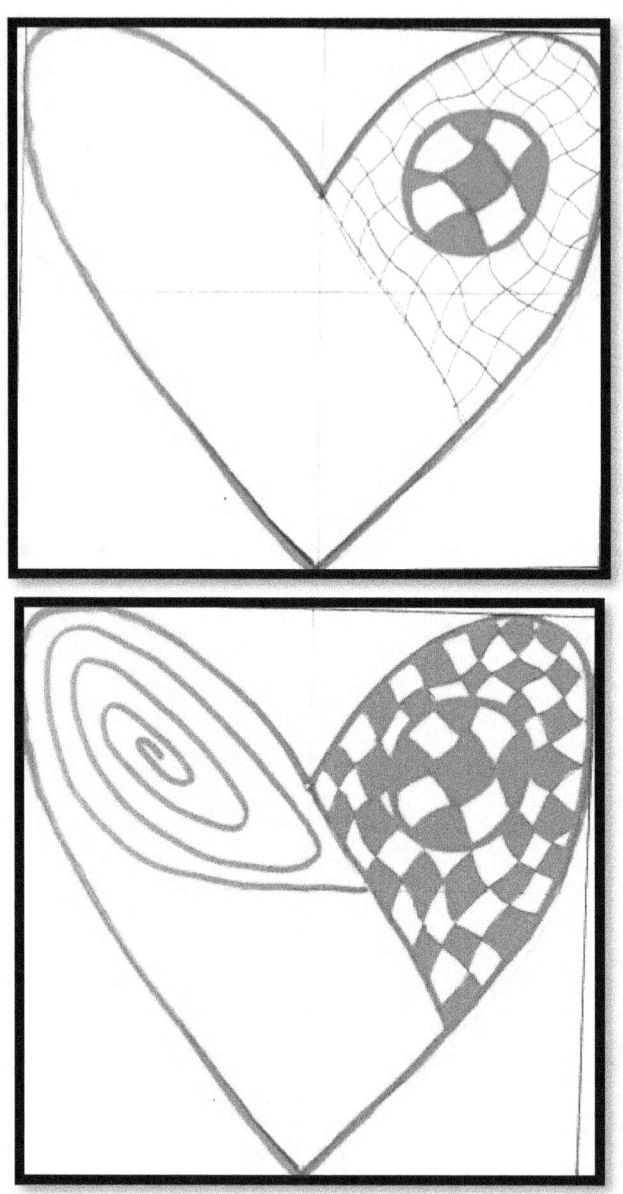

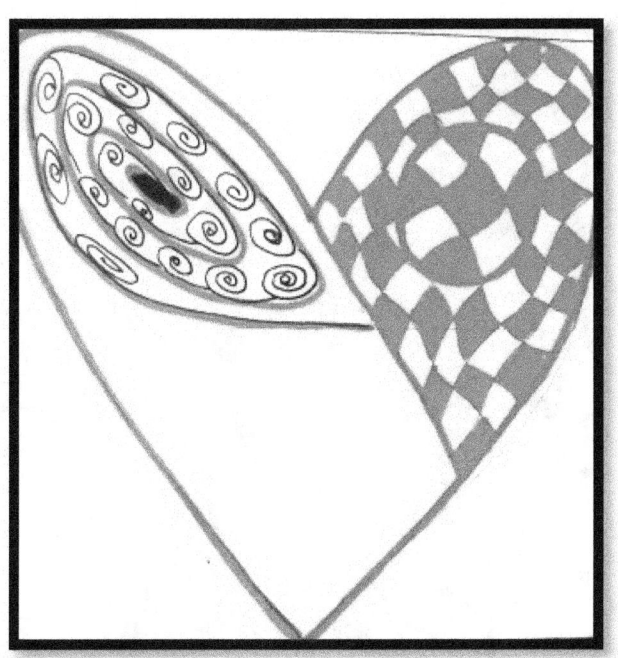

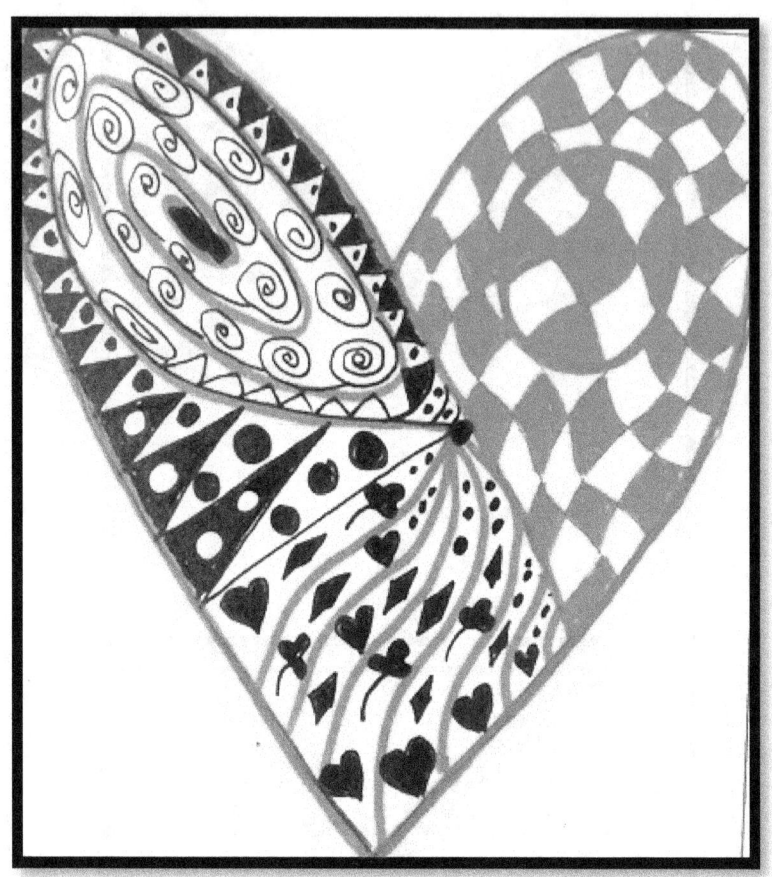

Conclusion

As I said in the introduction to this book on Zen art drawing, you'll find many more explanatory pictures of drawings than the text itself. Sometimes the text is not even needed, or to a lesser extent, to explain the procedure. You can easily figure out how to draw if you have the method "drawn".

I hope you've learned a lot about the Zen art of drawing from the book "Zen Doodling", and most of all I hope that you had a really good time. If you liked the first part of the book, then you will surely like the other one which will contain more tricky and inventive Zen drawings.

Thank you!

Thank you for choosing our book, we hope you found it interesting and helpful.

If you liked the book, please give us a favor to write your review.

We would really appreciate this!

If you would like to have a bonus – **FREE BOOK**, please send the screenshot of your review to this e-mail: **kelly.artbooks@gmail.com** and we will send you a **FREE BOOK** in PDF as a **GIFT!****

Hope to see you in our future books and good luck in your drawing experience!

** in the e-mail subject please mention the name of the book you reviewed and the author.

www.ingramcontent.com/pod-product-compliance
Lightning Source LLC
Chambersburg PA
CBHW070809180526
45168CB00002B/549